Sista!

Published January 2018 by Team Angelica Publishing,
an imprint of Angelica Entertainments Ltd

Team Angelica Publishing
51 Coningham Road
London W12 8BS

TEAM
ANGELICA

www.teamangelica.com
A CIP catalogue record for this book is available from
the British Library

ISBN 978-0-9955162-4-3

Printed and bound by Lightning Source

Supported using public funding by

LOTTERY FUNDED | ARTS COUNCIL ENGLAND

Sista!

AN ANTHOLOGY OF WRITINGS BY SAME GENDER LOVING WOMEN
OF AFRICAN/CARIBBEAN DESCENT WITH A UK CONNECTION

TEAM
ANGELICA

From the Editors

It's incredibly moving to be presenting this wonderfully diverse anthology of stand-out writing by and about same gender loving women (including bi, pan and non binary women) of African/Caribbean descent (including mixed race women) with a UK connection. Within these covers you will find poems of love and desire, longing and loss, trauma and triumph, of biological family and found/claimed family; autobiographical pieces sharing both difficulties and the joy and power to be found in overcoming them; histories personal, social and political; tales of love from both elders/foremothers and up-and-coming youth; affirmations of carefree singledom, loving coupledom and community; and lively, page-turning tales with women-loving black female protagonists at their centres. We hope they speak to you, move you, inform you, entertain and surprise you; and perhaps empower you to set down your own experience in writing – so much gets lost for want of being recorded, the more so for those who come from undervalued places and identities.

When we began this project – the sister volume to Team Angelica's landmark 2015 *Black & Gay in the UK* men's anthology – we found few predecessors. Perhaps the most well-known were from the USA – *Afrekete: An Anthology of Black Lesbian Writing* (Anchor Books 1995, ed. Catherine E. McKinley) and *Does Your Mama Know?: An Anthology of Black Lesbian Coming Out Stories* (Redbone Press 1998, ed. Lisa C. Moore). Closer to home we found the UK-based interview collections *Making Black Waves* (Scarlett Press, 1994, eds. Valerie Mason-John and Ann Khambatta) and its successor, *Talking Black – Lesbians of African/Caribbean/Asian Descent Speak Out* (Cassell, 2000) – see Valerie's reflections on publishing these in this book. More recently – again from the States – there's been *Lez Talk: A Collection of Black Lesbian Short Fiction* (BLF Press 2016, eds. S. Andrea Allen and Lauren Cherelle); but other than that there's nothing more recent than seventeen years ago, and those earlier titles are mostly out of print and hard to find. The world has changed a great deal since then, and so, while honouring the past, this anthology very much speaks to the now.

We set no parameters for our contributors, beyond asking for writing that touched on some aspect of being a same gender loving woman of African/Caribbean descent with links to the UK, and were delighted by the variety of responses we received, both in form and content; and were excited to receive work exploring in very different ways, and from very different cultural and social locations, so many aspects of intersections of identity, self-perception and experience. Choices about the capitalisations of words such as 'Black', 'Lesbian', 'Feminist' and others remain each author's own.

Thank you to all our writers for their hard work, their talent, their patience as we got the book together, and for their sharing of themselves. And thank you to you, the reader now holding this volume in your hands: we hope you enjoy it.

Phyll Opoku-Gyimah
Rikki Beadle-Blair
John R Gordon

Table of Contents

there is keloid scarring where they join, bruises where they overlap. my intersections ache...

P.J. Samuels

Remi Graves: 6 poems

Strong

To grip your hips as you bend, opening the oven—
to press myself not quite into you, but close—
is to know exactly who I want
and still be shadow-boxing the shape of such muscular lust.

I grapple with the thought of holding you tighter.
In the midday light, when it is impossible not to glimpse
the tree trunk shadow my body casts over yours
when I am just a branch, made strong by what is heavy:
the guilt of wanting you the way they say men do.

I'd like to shut my eyes like you do,
let them roll back into silence and feeling,
swap the fears I have yet to name for
the taste of skin, lips and hot breath.

You pull the oven door shut.
I am still in awe
of the way you trap heat.

Treasure

after Terrance Hayes

'Prove it then,
lift up your top'
the boy said teetering on
the halfpipe's lip.
I'd laughed louder than I'd meant to
pushing my body on the deck
back and forth over a crack in the concrete.

On edge, I rode the silence
skirting around the no
in my dustbowl belly.
'It's obvious she's a girl'
another boy shouted
with his back bent away from us
sucking his legs up close to his chest,
lending his skateboard flight.

My hot face twisted into gratitude's shadow –
I pulled my T-shirt away from my body
made excuses about mama and tea time
and pushed off down the path,
leaving his words sticking to the air.

I think of the boy
who spoke for me then,
on hot evening tube rides
when stares at my chest
turn me into a blazing thumb
jutting out amidst the well shaped fingers.

These days
I button my shirts
all the way up,
my neck a treasure chest
of secrets.

Bone

A baby sits soft flesh content
housing one hundred more bones
in her body than any adult can.
Tough to think of all that hard and marrow
hiding in the folds of her supple frame.
She bends to fit the plump of her toes
into a wet mouth. Creased thighs smile:
playing hide and seek with the rigid.
Years will pass and these bones will disappear
fall away like teeth that know when
they are no longer needed
or fuse together
matter making one self out of two
or the milk: they say it
erodes bones from the inside out.
Lips wrapped innocent around a nipple
mother's milk turns her hard
and soft all at once   and what
is the beauty in ageing
if not the refusal to calcify
when every thing asks
bone of you

poem to myself, based on a drawing
by a three year old

I will draw you with no hands
away from the sizeable hole
you find yourself in,
with arms thin and underfed
because you believed the lies
you were told
about women with muscles.
Your face will be your body,
legs shooting out of your chin.

You talk like someone who knows more than they feel,
a person lost in synapses and the obscurity of cognition.

Your feet will be large, spade like with no toes,
eroded from all the walking away.

You have confused the dance of soil moving beneath
for the art of digging where you stand.
Afraid to unearth what roots you
and grapple with the compost,
scared of what may nestle beneath your nails.

I will draw you with no hands
to remind us that children can always tell
what we are hiding from and
that dirt is only lost soil.

At six years old

when Lisa Bonet's face cast its perfect light skin shadow across your screen, how your adult self imagined a future lover might cast up dregs of deep buried self hate, the taste of burnt ochre. When the only way you could imagine your touching skins was with you dipped in chalk. And in this baptism you dropped the 'innate feminine', grew a thing between your legs to ratify your desire. Built a town across your shoulders, broad and there enough to sustain the gift of invisible. You, a small black thing wanting to love lighty mclight like blondie mcblonde. Young enough to think the world sees you how you see yourself, old enough to flick the channel quick when your mother walks in. You, the small black thing playing with your three selves, before knowing any of their names.

Regeneration
After Sue Kwock Kim

My grandmother is
hard at work
renovating our Ghana house.
She guts the place
like tilapia fish,
installs a new fridge
to house Cokes and bitter
lemons. Lets a breeze
chase ghosts
from front door to back.
There are no stairs
only barred windows
that let the mosquitoes know
this is not their home.
A green damp climbs
the corner of the walls
and will not desist despite
fresh licks of paint.
She says nothing
of the rotting foundations.
Instead says this home
will house our futures
but from where I'm looking
across two continents
and sea and more sea,
I'm not sure they'll
fit.

Gray Akotey

Levels

I was 14 years old in school when I first discovered I liked girls. At the time I didn't understand the infatuations I had with other girls or why I felt the way I did about my English and Maths teachers. I was confused, and acted out in an odd and rebellious way to try and make sense of it all... I felt suffocated, angry, frustrated. I was a Christian girl whose beliefs conflicted with everything I felt. I suppressed the way I felt, tried to date boys as a way to blank it out, but it never helped. I wanted so desperately to talk about it but there wasn't anyone but friends from school. It was a low period for me because everything that I felt was 'wrong' according to how I was raised.

Fast forward five years to 19 years old and heading off to university. That was my moment of liberation. I needed to know if how I was feeling was real. It was there I kissed a girl for the first time, and for me the world made sense. I couldn't turn back at this point; how could I?

For so many years I've wanted to share my life with you, talk to you about what I was going through, but because of the lasting feelings I had upon your discovery, I've never felt I could tell you about anything in my life, and I didn't want to lie. So I kept my distance in the physical form and chose what I wanted to tell you about my life. I omitted so much over the years, stuff I really needed my mum and dad for. Instead, I learnt to depend on myself or lean on friends for the love and support I felt I could get.

I've wanted to tell you about my life, yet it felt like I was coming out all over again and I begrudged doing that. But the longer it was left, the longer I realised that there was more and more distance separating us.

The above is a snippet of the three-page coming out letter I wrote to my parents back in 2014. I wrote it over the course of six months, toying back and forth with saying too much or too little. I grew up in a strict Ghanaian Christian household, the oldest of three children, and this meant three things; 1) church is life, 2) the Bible is life and 3) prayer is life. Everything was spiritual and everything had meaning.

I was fourteen years old when my curiosity began, but couldn't really articulate it until I was about sixteen. Having been raised in the church basically meant that oftentimes I, along with many others, was subject to sermons from pastors or a special bishop from out of town preaching homophobia. Even at the time, and not completely understanding it all, I was made to believe that it was a sin.

So when my curiosity reached its peak, I felt troubled. I battled with not knowing who I could confide in to help me understand. I started to feel uneasy about going to church because, despite its welcoming aura, I feel the church is filled with the most hypocritical and judgmental people. There's so much reverence for reverends, pastors and preachers. You are made to believe everything they say without challenge. They are the Chosen Ones, with an almost mythical air about them – as if they could see into your soul and see your deepest, darkest secrets and bellow them from the pulpit for everyone to hear. That fear crippled me because the last thing I wanted was to embarrass my parents in front of people that had known us for years.

I eventually confided in a youth pastor who told me to pray on it. I prayed hard, yet I couldn't stop thinking about how much I wanted to kiss this girl I knew. The praying didn't help and the desire didn't go away. I eventually found solace in a friend at school who comforted me and really put my mind at ease, saying, 'I already knew you liked girls. It doesn't make a difference to me. I still love ya!'

I suppressed my feelings for the next few years, until after my A Levels. I had intentionally selected universities that were at least two hours' from London, because quite frankly I didn't want any auntie to catch me with my tongue down a girl's throat and hurry that information back to my mum. So I waited until I was at Coventry University to embark on everything I had stored up for all those years. Let's just say my first term was a wild one...! I was 19 when I first had any intimacy with a woman and knew that I wanted to do this again and again. The feeling was like no other...

When I came home after university at 22, the stains of my liberation were clear to see. My style had changed – I was embracing my boyish side more, and this caused my parents to look at me suspiciously. My mum eventually said to me one evening, 'I put it to you, you like girls. I put it to you that you are sleeping with girls.'

I wasn't ready. This felt like an interrogation that wouldn't go favourably. I denied it. About a week later my mum came back again, this time with my dad and armoured with the Bible. My mum uttered the same words, 'We put it to you that you're a lesbian. We put it to you that you are sleeping with girls.'

Deny, deny, deny, I thought as the floor beneath me started to shake from my fear. She said, 'Okay, let's go to your room.' She'd found the box of sex toys that I'd accumulated from university – the last thing I wanted my strict Ghanaian mother to find. She said, 'Take the box out and show your dad.' I was beyond mortified and couldn't bring myself to show him, so it was taken from me and I never saw it again. I was definitely shook.

From that moment, and for the next 3-4 months, I was in a form of conversion therapy. Every day I came home, I sat with my parents and read the Bible. My dad had obtained specific scriptures from the bishop from the head church branch in Ghana, and he used those to 'pray the gay' out of me. I conformed to what they wanted out of fear. I tried to recondition my brain to not think about or look at women, I grew my hair, dressed more feminine, and attempted to date a man and make my parents happy. All of this was futile, because less than a year later I was back with women.

I wasn't very discreet. My parents found out I was seeing someone new and offered me 'help'. 'We can get you help to battle this,' my dad said.

'I'm NOT crazy. I don't need help.'

I had to choose. Choose to be happy. Choose to take control of my mental health, my sanity.

I had to choose.

That was the last conversation we had about it until almost ten years later. I moved out, and as the years progressed the distance between my parents and myself widened. Even though communication remained, it got less and less.

Throughout my twenties I never felt afraid when I was with women and living my life: I just did ME. And I was certain that there were women like me out there; surely I couldn't be the only Black, Christian, West African lesbian in London? So I started a YouTube channel to reach out to others and document my experiences navigating the lesbian world, sharing my thoughts and feelings. I was beyond surprised (and still am) to discover that there were SO many women out there just like me. Some who reached out are still close friends today.

While I was busy navigating this world without much closeness with my parents, they were getting closer to the church and their faith. I fought for many years to make sense of my sexuality and my religion, and at one point I had to choose. I had to choose not to fight mentally about whether God loved me or I was an irredeemable 'sinner' because I didn't repent of my sexuality, and all those other yearning questions. At this time my dad was ordained and became a reverend, preaching on radio and at different churches. My mum became a pastor's wife and did her duty for the church also.

Self-love was paramount but it didn't come immediately. I had to learn to love myself and to be strong.

I was 31 when I decided to put an end to the uncertainty. I was sure my parents knew that I was a lesbian, that my attraction to women wasn't a phase, but perhaps couldn't broach the subject. So I began writing my coming out letter. I felt it was the best way for me to convey everything I felt honestly and without interruption. The point for me was not to try and change my parents, but to get them to acknowledge their lesbian daughter. Just 'acknowledge' – because I know acceptance is a long way off.

When my parents had read the letter, I waited for over a month before they felt to discuss things. I was certain they knew, given all that had happened before, but had wanted to take ownership and let the words come from me.

They responded with a united front: 'We will still love you, but don't want anything to do with that part of your life.'

I'd gotten my answer and I thought I would be fine with

their choice. But ultimately I love my parents, and being 'fine' is just a coping mechanism.

I'm now 34 and the relationship is still very tentative. I still get the looks of disappointment or disapproval and they reduce me to being fourteen again. I realise that so much time has passed, and that I have grown and changed so much that being 'fine' is no longer okay. Mum is having dramatic spiritual dreams that mean I need to 'accept JC as your Lord and Saviour…' Dad and I talk, but only barely.

I understand that now I need to be the bigger person and break the years of silence. The concoction of staunch spiritual values clashes with worldly liberal ones, and when you add in the effects of colonialism it doesn't mix well. I need to show my parents love, and open the floor for more conversation. Maybe we can come to an understanding, maybe we won't. We are either in each others' lives wholeheartedly, or not. And that's the crossroads. I have to decide what's going to make me happy and, in turn, perhaps make them happy too. But to not live with regret, I will have to communicate.

I think that this whole 'coming out' thing is like beating the levels in a video game. Level 1 is plucking up the courage to tell your parents; Level 2 is do they accept it or not, and if they do you proceed to Level 3; if they don't, you have to stay and beat the Boss and escape to Level 4. As millennials we have to change that. Change the narrative of being Black, African and gay. Stop allowing others to label same gender loving as a sin. Love freely, openly and without concern. There are queer Muslims and gay Christians and as people we aren't clones. We aren't all made to be straight, cisgendered. And that's okay.

I'm strong and passionate. I love hard and with intent. I am me, flaws and all. I choose happiness, and accept all the love and light into my life.

Hopefully, the next level is where I beat the Boss.

Wish me luck for Level 4.

Kesiena Boom

Not White, Not Ever: a Black Lesbian Lament

Part One: Not White, Not Ever

In the infancy of my intimacies with other women, I was naive about the impact that race could have on my relationships. I was at university, freshly emancipated from the shackles of suburbia and learning every day to be more courageous and intentional about my lesbian identity. I was enamoured with the idea of lesbian solidarity and sisterhood, and truly believed that being bound together as women-loving women was enough to see any passionate relationship through. I dated and slept with a series of wholly inappropriate white women who interrogated and undermined my race and my anti-racism, and in the process sliced away my sanity one thin sliver at a time. I let them get under my skin, let their white sensibilities – obsessed with preserving the status quo – seep in and pacify me. There is a rootlessness to the reality of life as a mixed-race Black lesbian and I was desperate to grow roots, to curl them through the dirt and keep me fixed fast in place. I wanted to feel anchored and secure – a feeling I'd not had much experience of as one of the only Black kids and the only queer person of colour at my suburban Midlands school.

As I progressed through my degree in sociology at two different universities in two different cities, I became increasingly disheartened by my inability to harmoniously and contentedly form meaningful romantic relationships with white women. Eventually, after nearly a year in a committed relationship with a white woman, I realised that there were parts of me that I had been lessening, deadening, denying... and I could not do it anymore. I broke up with her because I knew that I could not bear to wake up in ten years' time, roll over in bed and think, 'there are parts of me you do not know'. I still loved her, but I knew that I didn't want to marry her, and I knew that I didn't want to have children with her. I still loved her, but I chose to put my true needs first. I needed to be seen in my entirety, without a suffocating white shroud laid over me.

I have loved white women and I have tried so very hard to push past our differences, to embrace the rhetoric of 'love overcomes'. I didn't want to accept and admit that sometimes that is just not true. There will always be separations and seas between us. Romantic love is not an abstract emotion, wrought from the ether. It is a co-construction between two people who must build that love from a place of mutual understanding and compassion for each other. And I knew that the love I could create with white women would always be missing some essential essence.

What would I stifle and stuff down if I committed my life to the emotional labour involved in soothing and protecting whiteness? What parts of me would become weak and worn from neglect? I knew that I did not want to find out. Compromise held no clarity for me.

As a teenager I once asked my mother, who is white, if she had ever considered the ramifications of having a child of a different race to her. A small pause blossomed and formed into a curt and dismissive, 'No, never,' tinged with a finality that let me know that even if I pressed the subject I wouldn't prise much more out of her. My mother is a formidably intelligent and accomplished woman, yet she suffers from an inability to discuss race and racism. Every time she flinches away from conversations about how our different positionalities as a white straight woman and a Black lesbian inform our lives, a desperate, needy part of me is wounded and bruised. And now it is always sore to the touch.

I never want my own brown child to have a conversation that falls anywhere close to those I had with my mother. Sat in the present, at twenty-two years old, my child is just a small hope far in the future, but even so, I cannot in good conscience let myself fall in love with a white woman. I cannot create the possibility that one day my child comes crying to me because her other mother has hurt a part of her through her lack of understanding.

And oh, is it not so easy to say 'not all white women', and is it not so easy to say that if I choose wisely I will not be hurt? But that is disingenuous and lacking. For as long as there are racial divides in this world that centre around Black dehumanisation, then there will be space for a white woman to hurt me and my small brown child, even if that child is also part of her. This is a lesson I have learnt with my own Black body, and this is a lesson I want my child to skip out on. I don't want to have a white child either. I don't want to raise a white child who will grow up to be more valued than the brown body she was pushed out of. I don't want to resent my own baby and I don't want her to see her mother experience something she will never understand. Even worse, I don't want to see her become tainted by white supremacy, so that I will never know if there is some part of her that sees me as Other or lesser, something to be ashamed of.

I hold deep resentment towards my own parents (despite my love for my mother), for throwing me together without a thought. I will hate my father forever for leaving his Blackness in me and then abandoning me to let me deal with it alone and with no guidance. We have never had a familial bond, and that can never be fixed. Black people have always had each other, that's how we've survived. But I had to learn to survive the hard way and I will not be part of perpetuating a similar cycle.

Part Two: The Desperation

I have never believed in soulmates. The idea that there is just one woman out there for me has always felt too close to the bone. As a lesbian, the dating pool is already very small. If one only wants to date other lesbians of colour with the same commitment to radical politics as oneself, then that pool shrinks and dries out until it is a sad, shallow puddle. The ramifications of this on my dating life have been significantly depressing. Whenever I do happen to meet another woman of colour who fulfils even some of the things I'm looking for, I am immediately far too invested. A small but persistent voice taunts me, If things don't work out with this woman, then what? What if she was the last one? What if I have doomed myself because I wasn't good enough, stable enough, smart enough, financially secure enough, interesting enough? What if I will always be alone because what I want is just... statistically improbable?

I once dated a girl who by some kind of miracle was also a half Urhobo, half white lesbian. Just like me. When I discovered that not only did we share Nigerian ancestry but that we were from the same tribe, I was delighted and overwhelmed. I had always resigned myself to the fact that being mixed-race meant the chances of me ever being with someone who had the exact same racial make-up as me were pretty much non-existent, and I'd made peace with that. But then this girl appeared in my life and she was so pretty and so talented and likable and she liked me too. I felt as though I had slipped into some sort of alternate universe in which romantic comedy-esque serendipitous surprises happened to mixed-race lesbians and not just to thin straight white girls. We dated for a couple of months and it was wonderful, but I knew from the off that we didn't have that elusive spark. I didn't want to give up though. I tried to kid myself that it might grow. I let myself ignore the fact that our personalities weren't massively romantically compatible. Instead I tried to focus on what we did have in common: our race, our love of writing... and that was about it. When she broke things off with me I was much more upset about the loss of my fantasy than the actuality of anything about our brief affair.

My best friend is white. They are a couple of years older than me, and they and their white girlfriend are in the process of starting to try to have children. They have found what they're looking for and though I could cry thinking about how happy I am for them, I could easily let those tears fall from a place of jealousy. The only queers I know who are engaged or who are planning families are white. The only queers I know who bounce from one satisfying relationship to the next are white. Lasting happiness and romance seem to be tied up in a tight, white bow that I will never be able to unravel. It's hard to not let bitterness harden my heart. I don't want to be that girl. I want to be able to enjoy other people's happinesses without fretfully fussing over the state of my own.

I can't even turn to my favourite form of escapism to dream of my queer brown future. There appears to be some kind of rule on TV that means that all lesbians of colour must have white partners. Is this to dilute them? Make them more palatable? More 'relatable'? Make them easier for the white gaze to glaze over? My favourite queer woman of colour on TV was Calliope Torres from *Grey's Anatomy*. All of her main love interests were white. She ends up having a child with a white man and marrying a white woman. She then leaves her wife and uproots her brown child from her home when she moves across the country to be with another white woman. Callie was magical and smart and beautiful and funny, but her entire romantic life revolved around whiteness. We never got to see what she would be like with a Latina girlfriend. We never got to see Callie's brownness affirmed by her partners. A cornerstone of lesbian culture is *The L Word*, which I have watched a baffling amount of times since first seeing it at sixteen, principally due to the fact that there is literally no other show which portrays lesbianism as its main focus for six whole seasons. Bette, one of the main protagonists, is a mixed-race Black woman. Her wife Tina is lily-white and largely clueless. When Tina is taken aback by the thought of carrying a Black child for Bette, I wished that Bette would up and leave. I longed for Bette to be with another smart, strong Black woman. I felt a deep, dark sadness for Tina's unborn Black child. I was desperate to see Black lesbians putting Blackness first, but I never did. You can't be what you can't see. What if I had seen what I needed and not spent years expending fruitless and frustrating energy on trying to bend to whiteness? It is a particular kind of cultural violence to see that the only love queer women of colour can find is with white women who water us down, wet our edges.

Part Three: Contentment

I know that if I want to salvage my sanity, I must begin to come to terms with the possibility that I may never find a wife. Queerness dissolves opposites, it lessens the false dichotomies of the world, those that state a woman must have a man and rationality cannot exist alongside emotionality and blood is thicker than water. Or even that a woman must have a woman. So, then, I must look to my queerness to accept that the opposite of married is not alone and the opposite of a relationship is not loneliness. I need to trust in my bonds with my chosen family and in my bond with myself.

I know that I must try to reconcile reality with the lies and artifice of romance built by patriarchy. The myths of patriarchy, which keep it alight, tell women that they will one day find a man who fixes their place in the world. Queer women are not immune from the myths of romance, the inevitable 'solves-it-all' woman just waiting to appear around the corner. I need to know that I can turn round that corner and just keep walking, head held up high, alone but not lonely.

I will not eulogise my hope of finding the perfect partner just yet, but I also will not let myself mourn the future I may never have. I know I have the strength to resist relationships that will eat me from the inside, and I know that whatever happens I will find a way to be okay. I want to look at the woman I love and know that she will know, without a word passing between us, the peculiar pain of being Other three times over: Woman, lesbian, Black. Yet if that day never comes to pass, I shall weave myself into tight rope, taut against all storms. I will anchor my own damn self and I will be free.

Eileen Bellot

Splinters

How many ya'll remember Splinters?

The black hairdressers situated in the heart of the West End, giving us blacks a modern, funky destination. It stated our arrival; that our hair was prestigious enough for a style centre of its own in 1980s London. Our manes – both male and female – were styled and fashioned into wet looks, relaxes, and cutting-edge shapes by our Brothas and Sistas, to the backdrop of music that was our own. UK bands like Hi-Tension bringing us into the '80s with the British Hustle and Loose Ends, creating an RnB flavour that didn't look to the US for approval. This was a decade that saw the launch of a confident Black British identity right across hair, music, fashion and attitude. We were starting to accept the fact that 'back home' was a long way away from England, and it wasn't necessarily going to be our home. As a young design student – at the London College of Fashion, I might add – I felt I had arrived, and it was befitting that I should be crowned by the people at the forefront of black radical hairstyling.

In contrast, the '70s was a time where mainstream culture dominated references. If there was a black person on TV you would get a phone call from at least 4-5 relatives within seconds, alerting you to '…turn the telly on – there's a black person on telly!' It was a major event to see our likeness represented on mainstream media then. As a young black teenager there were two looks to choose from, both referenced by black music. If you liked reggae you were a Casual and wore Farrah slacks and Gabicci knitwear. Or if you were into Soul music you were a Soulhead, and the clothing was more colourful and less restricted. I'm sure you can guess I was a Soulhead.

My hair was what my peers and elders called 'good hair' or 'coolie hair'. As a child in the playground, unlike my friends, I didn't have to mimic our white counterparts' hair by wearing a cardigan over my head. My locks were naturally fine, long and flowing. This was at least a decade before imported American hair products could bestow Rapunzel-like European tresses upon anyone who was prepared to pay for them. In the '80s fine, long black hair was still considered a prize gift to be revered. It did, however, use to annoy me when I tried to get an afro; I would spend hours back-combing it, then get outside and with one gush of wind it would be flat again.

So there I was in the '80s, wanting something different from the usual styles and fashions which I could push, pin or braid my natural hair into. Where better to turn than Splinters? I didn't need hot iron combs to straighten my hair like my mum and sisters, or want to go to bed with a headful of hair rollers to get curls. The latter just wasn't the look for any discerning fashion designer. Like many of my more contemporary peers, I opted for a wet look. My mum laughed at me for spending so much money on getting my wet-look perm, and would tease me by saying, 'You dunno you got good hair? You jus' wasting your money giving dem people. Jus' use de cream and your hair will curl. You got good hair!'

For a year or so I was happy to just have the perm and a trim, and then follow-up visits to sit under the steamers to treat my hair. Remember those bloody heavy, cumbersome steamers? They were like space helmets, only ten times bigger. One day I got bored and told my hairdresser – Terry, I think his name was – to give me a cut that was different: I felt daring.

Too afraid to let go of my hair length, I opted for a trim to the sides that still allowed my hair to retain its length at the back – and me a safe re-entry into Hackney, where I would have to deal with the local black girls giving the 'I dunno who she thinks she is' glare. If they thought I was weird they should have come to my college to see I was a tame lion in comparison to what everyone else was wearing! Wow, I was dead pleased with my cut; I could feel the breeze around my ears. On my way home I gazed at myself in every shop window or glazed surface I came across. I was now amongst the elite Avant Garde Black Britons. After all I was never one of those black girls into reggae, going clubbing at Cubies and All Nations – I was stepping out at the Wag Club or Heaven. With my new crown in place, I could now fully claim my title as a Fashion Designer. Not just a Hackney gal – but a West End Girl!

As the bus took me home, my head started to shrink back

down to size at the thought of my mum's reaction to me having cut my hair. What would she say, what would she do? I got off the 22 bus a few stops earlier than usual and took the long walk down Chatsworth Road to give myself time to work out how I was going to enter the house. I arrived at the door, my daring haircut declaring my stake for independence and claim to adulthood. But I knew my mum had a way of reminding me and my siblings whose house it was and who was in charge. I grabbed a hat from my bag, pulled it over my head, turned the key in the lock and entered as fast as I could, shouting, 'Good evening!' as I ran up the stairs to the sanctity of my bedroom. My younger sister Cathy took one look at me and said, 'Has Mum seen you yet?'

I was up there for a nerve-wrecking two hours before my mum called us down for dinner. In those two hours I managed to convince myself that it was 'only a little trim' and Mum probably wouldn't notice anyway. More fool me!

'What de hell you go and do to your hair – you cut it!? De one good thing I give you and you cut it!' She sucked her teeth so hard and long I thought she might have swallowed them. But she wasn't finished with me. 'You mean to tell me you dunno dat your hair is your beauty! You dunno de story of Samson and Delilah!? – You go let dem people cut off your strength and beauty!'

She felt mortally wounded that I had dared to cut away the one thing about me that was her pride and joy. To her my hair was my birthright, passed down from my ancestors. She just couldn't understand why I would want to cut even a centimetre off, never mind shave the sides. She stomped off and didn't talk to me for a whole week.

Poor mum, I can see her face now: she was so hurt. Looking back, it was really the beginning of me claiming myself. She'd be rolling in her grave if she could see my hair today. I have dispensed with hairdressers and now take to the barber's weekly, for a Number One!

...my sister
love you a woman.
hard.
love her in the morning,
afternoon and evening.
love her every second
in between.
love every cell
of her being,
with every atom
of your existence.
love you a woman.
hard.
and I pray
that woman is you.

P.J. Samuels

Jennifer Daley

A Dutch Pot of Identity

As a kid I remember my dad's Dutch Pot on the kitchen stove, simmering away with curried goat and cowfoot. Invariably next to it would be a frying pan sizzling with Mum's egg-and-bacon fry-up. I liked both, but would always opt for the frying pan if I had a school friend over for tea.

As a biracial child growing up in a predominantly white environment in the 1980s, I was acutely aware of my difference from a young age. I became skilled at learning how to assimilate and 'iron out' both the social – and literal – kinks in order to assimilate with my peers.

With a white British mother and a black Jamaican father, I was born with a full head of thick, curly black 3B hair. Throughout childhood I longed for the long, flowing, smooth hair of my shiny, carefree white school friends, and had a daily battle with my outward-growing frizz, which – along with my thick National Health glasses and braces – attracted taunts from the school bullies and made my life a self-conscious daily grind.

Playing out fantasies at home, I would steal a net curtain from the laundry basket and attach it to my head with hair grips, in order to fleetingly feel the liberation which I thought differently-shaped follicles would afford me. One summer I decided to take notes from the only two black kids in my area and work with my natural hair texture, rather than against it. Perhaps embracing my 50% African DNA (by way of a chemical process) was the key to finally feeling at home in myself and gaining acceptance from two new potential allies. So on a Saturday morning in 1991 I dragged my mum across town and spent my birthday money on a Jheri Curl perm. I was going to feel beautiful at last – I could hardly wait.

Stopping off at the only Afro Hair & Beauty supply shop within a twenty mile radius, I emptied the shelves of the requisite grease and hair oil needed to maintain such a hairstyle.

On my return home, I found myself in a hinterland of identity.

Weighted down by the rich emollients, my crown was now displaying a flat, lank and lifeless hairdon't. Rather than giving it the sheen, lushness and vivacity I'd hoped for, I was left with a randomised array of de-elasticised, depressed, wavy-straight strands.

This feeling of 'otherness' delayed my foray into the world of teen romance and dating, to the point that sexual relationships were avoided completely until my early twenties. Until that point I had assumed I was only attracted to boys, though had little to go on save for a few snatched and embarrassed kisses in high school.

In the summer of 2002, I found myself about to embark on my first same sex relationship.

It was with gay female colleague, to whom I had fostered a curious but intense attraction in the months previous, and turned out to be the kind of disastrous, messy, traumatic yet transformative affair that often characterises first loves. Several similarly fun, instructive and dramatic affairs followed successively, involving a roughly equal ratio of men to women. I started attending queer events and found myself at a brand new intersection – subtly neglecting to mention if I was currently dating a man, for fear of invalidating my seat at the table. Having the privilege of being able to exist comfortably in a heteronormative environment, I noticed a correlation between my biracial identity and my sexual orientation. With two feet in four worlds, I had no idea how to integrate them all.

The next twelve years took in the death of my father, a failed trip to Jamaica, and a painful but ultimately rewarding 'coming out' to my mother in order to be able to understand and celebrate all the different experiences that my racial and sexual identity have given me. And also to know that although both of these social constructs affect how I am received by the world, so are they constantly evolving and being redefined. Just as my preferences may be affected by time, so too are cultural and societal definitions of race.

We're all on a continuum. And I'm finally happy to be there.

P.J. Samuels

RADICAL

The fact that the only way a black woman can own herself is to be willing to be considered radical, is to be political, is an indictment of this world, and a further addition to the burden of being black and female. I never chose to be political. I have never thought of myself as radical. I am soft. So soft. I simply chose to own the body life gave me, own being racialised black, and revel in the beauty of my existence unapologetically. I am my hair, wherever on my person it grows. I may keep it, I may remove it, but my beautiful is not wrapped up in it. I am my skin. I am my voice, my accent, my heritage. I own the gender I was assigned at birth and I push back against all pre-packaged vulnerabilities, some after I had already suffered. I am what I look like, how I present, what you see, as much as I am who I am inside. This body is how I interact with the world and how I house being human, and my spirit gleefully declares this is home to me. My body is not irrelevant. A world that teaches me that to be truly spiritual is only about what I am inside is hostile. The violence and erasure that tries to teach me I am not my body is passively aggressive. My body matters. It is subjected to your unfettered gaze, and after you strip me and tear me to shreds with your standards, you tell me you need to see my soul so you can KNOW me, BEFORE you can appreciate me. The answer to that is no. My soul is not on offer. You have already taught me how you love by how you treat my very present and highly visible body. This body is how I interact with the world and how I house being human. What I am inside is only available to me. My very visible body is available to your gaze. I do not have a choice about that. I should not be obligated to also make my inner being available in order to get your appreciation. My body matters. My person is beautiful. My physical person. My spirit is mine. I have never volunteered to be political. I am not particularly strong, except I have no option. I am not particularly confident, I just believe in choice and personal autonomy. I am not particularly stubborn, I just know what I believe in and why, and fitting in is not an adequate reason to give up my beliefs and adopt others. I am not particularly open, I just refuse to participate in a notion of privacy that is a curtain behind which I and other women suffer abuse and injustices. I am not ashamed. I am not your shame. Feel your feelings but I will neither embody them for you, be your priest to receive your confession and absolve you, nor be the person you can outsource your guilt to. I am always conflicted when complimented on how beautifully I occupy an existence I never chose, an existence I often forget I embody. In my mind I am just plugging along with survival, taking my joys where they find me. There is this constant need to explain my very existence as if my continuance is an enigma. How dare me be alive and black, black and alive, alive and living abundantly; poor, black, female and vibrantly alive. How dare me? The thrill of being mundane is enough. I am happy. That, ostensibly, is terrifically radical.

Rue Gumbochuma: 3 poems

My mother's peach tree

What kind of peach tree doesn't ripen?
Are you damaged at the root?
Continuously bearing stubborn fruit
Ignorant of season
Existing without reason
Have you lost all hope or meaning?

What kind of peach tree are you?
Every day my brother asks for you
As if I am your keeper
I promised him a fruitful summer
Not knowing I had to question you as a provider

You remind me of my father

What kind of peach tree doesn't ripen?
Have you seen the peach tree next door?
Rumbi says it already tastes much sweeter
Are you not tired of being mediocre?
If it wasn't for my mother
I would've just cut you down and started over

What kind of peach tree are you?
Maybe your seeds were tainted
You were planted
in a corner of a garden that became a forest
Perhaps the light couldn't reach your branches
Do you blame the dark or its creations?
Are you just an inevitable manifestation?

What kind of peach tree doesn't ripen?

I sat on your shoulders
Bending your back backwards
Picking each peach
Patience
Was never something I owed you.

Great Zimbabwe

My mother is Great Zimbabwe
stones and ruins
remaining past stones and ruin

My mother is chrome and diamonds
forged from a mine bordering Botswana
forged from a dime that stood as a grandmother

My mother is the Bantu and Chi Karanga
You hear in my tongue
even when I'm speaking this non-native tongue

My mother is Robert Mugabe in 1981
She is the freedom that rained
flooding Dzimba Dzemabwe into Rhodesia

My mother is the wailing songs of hope
you hear echoed from each end of the Zambezi
and whispered by each forest tree

My mother taught Victoria how to fall
and I'll tell you why I believe that story;
I once saw my mother fight off a whole tribe

I once saw my mother run miles
bearing a whole village
better than she was God sent

Give me the pain of being broken-hearted by a girl
than seeing my mother fall
that's an easier poem

My mother is now a British summer
plagued by light rain
and passive aggression

My mother is a dimly lit airport runway
bodies stacked side by side

taking me home

My mother is a beach in Wales
My mother is the world cup
football bets in William Hill

My mother is an NHS waiting room
labour choked nurses
and conservative doctors who show no zeal at bad news

my mother is
Great.

Time

I will stop loving you, tomorrow
Your lips will be a brisk wind
Your kiss will be a bruise
And your tongue, a poem

I will stop loving you, tomorrow
Your grip will be limp
Your hair, a distant memory
I will no longer feel your fingertips against my hip

I will stop loving you, tomorrow
Your name will be a book
Your words, sold to the highest bidder
Your letters, only remembered in a bonfire

I will stop loving you, tomorrow
Your voice will be an echo
Your taste, a faint mango
Your body, an antique I used to own

I will stop loving you, tomorrow
I will remember you on occasion
You will be reduced to an urban legend
Just a collection of stories I tell at dinner parties

A phase
A midlife crisis at twenty-three
A disfigured photograph
A perfect example of what shouldn't last

If I stop loving you
I will cling onto greener pastures
and neglect our time spent faster
than you said, 'I love you'

I will not return
Time will not stand still
And I will simply
Stop.

Joy Gharoro-Akpojotor

Dakota

Dear Diary,

Today, 19ᵗʰ December 2014, is the day that Love died.

It died in the most spectacular way. I saw bright shining lights, fireworks, heard wailing from across the shores. There was a band that played all night long as the little children danced in circles, as the adults quietly held hands, mesmerised by the sight in front of them. Love was gone. In its place it left lust, nothing more than ashes lingering around. The women flashed their eyes at each other, suggestive looks that showed now they were free to do as they pleased. The rules had changed: there was no chance that this could be more than what it was, a bit of fun to let your urges be released, to have the tingle between your thighs licked. This was a new day.

Let me explain to you, Dear Diary, how I killed love. I killed it by telling it what it was, smothered it until it could not breathe anymore, its flame slowly disappearing to nothingness.

I first met her in 2012, the year of the Olympics. People were thrilled it was on home turf; me, I just wanted to have space back. Too many people were in town, too many feet around, too many hands in the air, too many voices when I stepped out the house; it was just a whole lot of too many. A person cannot think when there's just too many happenings around, and I needed my space. I'd found a quiet spot, or maybe the spot found me – sometimes the Universe just gives us things so that we remember what is important to us.

I've never liked people, I prefer my space. I've always been that way, ever since I was a child. My mother used to worry about me; she thought I was going to grow up a loner. I don't think there's anything wrong with just wanting to be on your own. If you can't live with yourself how are you going to live with other people? I needed to find somewhere that allowed me to be by myself, to allow my thoughts to wander freely without constraints, and you can't do that when people are constantly trying to talk to you; asking you for directions as if Google wasn't invented for that; asking for advice on where to eat, who to eat, how to eat; it's too much.

Anyway, I stumbled upon this place whilst I was walking along the canal towards Little Venice. It was by a tree. The stumpiest tree that I ever did see, but it offered shade and seemed somehow noise-proof. For the first week I would go there and sit beneath this tree, let it cover me in its glory whilst I read or ate or just watched particles of life pass me by. I named my tree Dakota.

One day whilst I was at Dakota, this tall shadow engulfed me. I opened my eyes and I saw the most stunning silhouette ever. She was breathtaking. Her dark skin was perfect. It was like she was from another planet. She was perhaps my age, twenty-something. Her natural hair was carefully pulled back into a bun, and when she spoke, she spoke with an international accent – I couldn't place where she was from, but as I would soon learn, it wasn't really an accent from anywhere. She wore a flowing summery dress that showed off her strong arms. She was magnificent and here I was unprepared in my black T-shirt and combat shorts – at least I got a fresh trim today.

'You're at my tree,' she said. Her voice was deep and sultry, it was a melody but it was harsh. It stung and healed me all at once. As I stared at her I struggled to find my words; it was as if she took them from me and wouldn't give them back.

'I said you're at my tree,' she repeated.

I finally found my words. 'Your tree?'

'Yes, my tree.'

'But I've been coming here for a week and I've never seen you before.'

'I've been on holiday. A girl is allowed a break now and again.'

'I don't dispute that, but I don't think this tree belongs to anyone; there's nothing on it that says it belongs to you.'

'Well, I'm telling you it belongs to me. You see that house over there?' She pointed at a house at the end of the road. I say 'house', but it had two turrets at the front. I should have guessed she was a princess of something, I mean someone this beautiful, she probably owned all of the land I was sat on.

'Yes, I can see it,' I replied.

'Well, that's where I live.'

'Who are you?'

'I'm the person that owns this tree.'

'Can't we share it? It's the only quiet spot I've been able to find.'

She looked me up and down, inspecting me, checking to see if I was a safe person or not. Then she smiled at me. 'Yes, we can share the tree, on one condition.'

'What's that?'

'Promise not to fall in love with me.'

I laughed out loud. She sure did have some nerve thinking that I was going to fall in love with her, who the hell was she?

'You've got a deal.'

We shook hands on it. Her hand was soft; she hadn't worked a day in her life. Her long, elegant fingers slipped easily into mine. I enjoyed feeling her skin on mine. I moved over a little and she sat beside me.

Every day for the next three weeks we would sit side by side under Dakota and talk. We talked about the stars, the distance between space and time, the meshing of worlds. We talked about history and the future, about what life meant, who we were. We spoke about the present and how nothing is as it seems; about the world and how the Universe is so much more than what we think or know; alternate dimensions. We experienced each other in a profound way that I had never felt before.

One afternoon, as we lay shaded from the harshness of the sun by Dakota's gently-stirring leaves, I turned to her and asked, 'Why can't I fall in love with you?'

'Because I cannot love you back.'

'Why not?'

'Because Nanaya made it so.'

'Nanaya? Who – what – is that?'

'Who she is doesn't matter. I am here to help others love, but not to love. I am here to show what love can be, but not to give the love. I am here to help others believe in love and the good that it can do. But love in the wrong hands can be destructive.'

'Has your love been destructive?'

'Perhaps.'

'How?'

'I don't know when to stop. What is the point of love if you end up killing what you cherish the most?'

'The point of love is that you experience it,' I said. 'Look around you. All of this will be gone sooner or later. All that will be left is us, our souls roaming the galaxies looking for other vessels to inhabit. We love so that we can feel.'

'And when the people you love are gone? When they die? When they decide that they don't love you anymore? What then?'

I gently cupped her face in my hands.

'Then we love again.'

I kissed her. Gently at first and then passion took control. Dakota covered us with her heavenly shade as we kissed and our souls touched each other for the first time. Diary, I'll try to explain to you what it felt like kissing her – it felt like there was an explosion inside my chest, like I had finally found what the meaning of life was – it was this moment. It felt as if my whole life had been created for this one singular moment, to be with her. So I held onto it with all of my might, I ate and drank it for breakfast, lunch and dinner.

Looking back now, I think I had a bit too much of it. At times it made me sick to my stomach. But I didn't care too much about that; I still kept on taking it all in. There were nights when I couldn't sleep because I had too much of her inside me, but it didn't matter: the urge was insatiable and I couldn't stop.

Then one day I went to Dakota to meet her, and she wasn't there. The next day she still wasn't there. Then the next and the next and the next. On the sixth day I walked over to the castle where she lived and knocked on the big doors. A butler answered. He said that they had been waiting for me to arrive. He led me into a large hallway. The air was warm and smelt of beeswax. At the far end were a great pair of golden doors. He knocked on them, three even raps, and the doors opened by themselves. He stood aside. I stepped into the room beyond and at once I was surrounded by stars and moons and planets that I had never seen before.

'Do you like what you see?' said a female voice behind me. I spun around and saw light floating in front of me in the shape of a woman. Her face was sculpted to perfection, her brown skin drew me towards her. She was so beautiful I began to cry. I had never seen a black woman as wonderful as her.

'Who are you? Where am I?'

'So many questions, so little time – my name is Nanaya, and you're in my home.'

'You have the universe in your house?'

'We all have the universe in our houses. I just choose to keep mine on show.'

I took in the sights around me once more, still in awe at what I was seeing, but I soon remembered why I had come. 'Where is she?'

'She's gone.'

'Have you taken her away from me because we love each other?'

'She decided that it was time to move on from this world.'

'Why?'

'Because love is destructive.'

'What are you talking about? Love is indestructible, it's the one force that transcends time and space, it can exist within one person or several people, it has no limitations!'

'But that is where you are wrong. Love does have its limitations. The ones that you placed on it. You told love what it could or couldn't be, how it could live, where it could live. You took love and placed it in a box.'

'I never placed her in a box.' I couldn't understand how she could just leave like that: we had something so rare that no one else but us could ever experience it, and she just took that away.

'You placed her in a box when you wanted her for yourself.'

'Where is she?'

'Somewhere out there. Now I have to go and find her.'

'Will you bring her back?'

'I don't know. Now that she's gone, the world will be different.'

'How different?'

'You'll have to figure that out for yourselves.'

'Can you give her a message for me?'

'Sure.'

'Tell her I only wanted to be with her, that was all.'

I walked out of that room filled with whirling galaxies, out of the castle. By the time I turned around, it had gone. I walked over to Dakota and sat under her.

Her shade was still there.

Yrsa Daley-Ward

Missing

I tried so many things to win you back,
a juicer, a gym, the old perfume,
indian hair,
a new cut,
collagen, reeboks, a cookery class
still,
you remained unmoved.

I took myself out for dinner
cried in front of my friends and their families,
drank gin,
drank gin
and
I drank gin,
looked foolish
stopped eating, wore less,
was cruel to my lovers
and all for
what

still I tried blood, offered up my collarbones, tested my liver
and that dark space at the back of my head, made space in
every last dream, heard our music in everything, felt sure you
were coming

felt damn sure you were coming

thought I saw you through my window

god, I
I think I
breathed less, took up less room
lost rhythm, forgot about my feet
painted my face grey,

spat out my reason
left questions in magazines,
smelled you gone most days, longed for your touch, especially
your teeth

(I would have given anything for your teeth)

left three letters with your doorman, harassed your mother,
smoked
your tobacco, coughed
and thought I saw you again for a moment,
my lungs ablaze, smarting.

....

You took a trip,
called the redhead back, bought me flowers, a computer, new
perfume
a harpsichord
and left them outside my door
where they stayed, in the rain
for one week

asked your mother to do her magic
with the moon and the oils
and the ocean
and the flowers.

She said those
dark ones are trouble
always wanting things out of their
reach.

(Your mother thinks
women
like me
are for learning on.)

You become fluent in parties
told everyone you loved me,
but it was just
too
hard,
stood in my garden
some early mornings
cried when you thought I might hear, gave up when I didn't.

You married her
I cant believe
you married her

trained the curl pattern out
of your hair
took pictures
heavy and smiling
with her family
your mum
and all of our friends

and all of your friends.

.

Phyll Opoku-Gyimah

Sistas Making It Happen

I am so glad I get to write for this amazing anthology, and that I get to write about the history and herstory of UK Black Pride (UKBP). I feel passionate, excited, pleased, sometimes saddened, but also motivated to share some knowledge about how UKBP started.

I'm going to get straight into it. With the month of June – Pride season here in the UK – upon us, I started writing this on 1st June, and I hope that I am able to articulate UK Black Pride's mission, its origins, why we exist, what we want to achieve, and how you, the reader, can get involved.

As the proud co-founder and Executive Director of UKBP, I was never under any illusion that setting up a Black Pride would not cause some sort of controversy in the UK, but my gosh, I wasn't ready for the anger, displeasure, division and hate that was thrown my way for daring to create a platform for Black, Black Asian Minority Ethnic (BAME/BME) People of Colour (PoC) and their friends to celebrate who we are, as well as challenge racism within our own LGBTQI+ communities – along with homophobia, biphobia, transphobia, Islamaphobia and other forms of discrimination that hurt our communities.

UK Black Pride's mission is to promote unity and co-operation among all Black people of African, Asian, Caribbean, Middle Eastern and Latin American descent, (as well as their friends and families), who identify as Lesbian, Gay, Bisexual, Transgender, Queer or/and Intersex.

We are committed to producing an annual celebration of Black Pride, as well as organising a variety of activities throughout the year in and around the UK which also promote and advocate for the spiritual, emotional, and intellectual health and well-being of all related communities. Our aim is to foster, present and celebrate Black LGBTQI+ culture in all its variety through education, the arts, cultural events and advocacy. UK Black Pride works closely with Paris Black Pride, as well as showing solidarity with other Black Prides in the USA and

Canada. Did you know that we only have two Black Prides in Europe, and that we have all faced the same challenges in terms of sponsorship, safe spaces, and around being able to see positive representation and visibility at well-established Prides, which don't always take intersectionality on board when planning their events?

So, a little bit of history of UK Black Pride. In 2004 I was an organiser for a brilliant online group called BLUK – Black Lesbians in the UK. BLUK was trying to take some of its activities off-line and create an atmosphere that fostered positive opportunities for networking and a sense of community for black lesbian, bisexual and trans women.

In August 2005 myself, Khi, Nixx and Bo (other leading lights at BLUK), arranged a social outing for our members to the sleepy seaside town of Southend-on-Sea in Essex. Why Southend? Well, many of the women going on this outing had not been outside of London since arriving in this country; also as a child I remember going to places like Southend, Margate and Broadstairs – we didn't have much money and couldn't afford to go abroad – and I love the seaside.

What began as a minibus trip to a nicely-secluded beach quickly developed into three coach-loads of lesbian, bisexual and trans Black women making the first of a long and proud journey that since then has grown in size and stature, and is all about inclusivity.

I don't think I can do that first trip justice here, but bloody hell, when I think back! I remember someone donating money to us to pay for a marquee; we hired a little sound system; we set up a volleyball net and brought along some other games like dominos. Someone called Angie Legs bought along her jerk pan and looked after the food as well as mixing some strong rum punch. We held a competition called Mr & Miss Beach, with prizes for the best-dressed couple, best swimwear and boldest modelling off. We had performances, speakers like Linda Bellos, and Earl Folkes from the USA, and not to mention DJs spinning the best tunes and everyone dancing to the 'Candy'.

I'm feeling really emotional writing this, because what no one could have foreseen was that that event was the start of history and herstory for the black/bme/poc community in

Britain when it came to shaping our pride movement.

It was in 2005 that I turned to Bo and said, 'This feels like Black Power and Pride. I want to make this happen all the time.' Bo said that she could see me doing amazing things now and in the future, and that she too was excited about this. I do not often gloat, show off or require the limelight, but that day I was so inspired, charged and ready to be a change-maker alongside people like Nixx and Khi. I know that I am a natural born organiser and someone who will be at the forefront of a liberation struggle. My mother is an organiser, so was my grandmother, and my great grandmother was a changemaker too. So you see it's in my blood to organise for change.

Everyone – especially the sistas – involved in making sure we had an amazing time at BLUK in 2004, and then taking it into 2005 so that we could feel connected and empowered in organising that first event, I cannot thank you enough from the bottom of my heart. I am inspired by every single one of you and I know that I've said that directly to you. And now I'm proud to say it here.

So there you have it: Black Pride was born out of the hard work and dedication of black lesbians, bisexual and trans women – people of colour. Not many know that, but for me it's important that it is known, and so I record it here.

During the build-up to that one incredible outing to South-end the concept of a Black Pride organization and annual event evolved through discussion, planning, and speaking to some of the elders in our community. The UK Black Pride event that followed was a success, and since then UKBP has grown year on year as a space where LGBTQI+ PoC can foster a sense of pride in our identities.

It is also worth noting that it was in 2005, when there was a surge in electoral support for racist and homophobic Far Right political extremists, that I would say members of the Black LGBTQI+ communities in Britain decided the time for waiting was over. We needed full support from both the Black/BAME and the LGBTQI+ communities, and we needed it immediately. And so it was that UK Black Pride came into being, with a mission to combat endemic racism and homophobia inside and outside our communities – as well as tackling other expressions of discrimination that touched our members.

Another major factor was about not seeing ourselves represented in the mainstream LGBT+ movement generally, or in Prides around the country – in London, Manchester, Brighton, Birmingham and others. Of course some things are changing, but it really felt like the mainstream movement didn't reflect the diversity in our communities. It didn't speak to us, nor did it feel like us, and it was not reflective of the real issues we needed to discuss. In a lot of cases that is still true today.

So what do you do when you don't see yourself somewhere? You can go into a dark, soul-destroying place, or you can create the change you want to see.

On 18th August 2006, I, along with a brilliant team, ensured the UK Black Pride event was etched into LGBTQI+ history as the leading celebration of African, Asian, Caribbean, Middle Eastern and Latin American LGBT+ people from Britain, Europe and internationally. We also laid the foundations to ensure that UK Black Pride becomes a permanent feature on the annual calendar of Pride activities.

We have grown from strength to strength because we have continued to secure the confidence, respect and support of the community, our friends and families. I certainly believe that we have maintained the core essence of being the only Black LGBTQI+ community Pride event to be genuinely designed, delivered and led by the full diversity of LGBTQI+ people of colour, and this is something I am immensely proud of.

Whilst this all sounds wonderfully positive, and in many ways is, there were also tears, heartache, stones thrown, and a lack of respect from certain quarters of our own LGBT+ communities. UK Black Pride members were told to F*** Off out of meetings and go back to where we came from; sponsorship was given to big and well-established Prides who wouldn't even give us the crumbs from the table; mainstream LGBT+ media would not even cover our activities, and we were called 'racist, separatist and discriminatory' for creating an event to ensure we could celebrate who we are in what was our own safe, not-for-profit, non-commercialised event, led by the community and for the community.

As one of my fellow UK Black Pride directors said, 'To us

Pride isn't just a celebration, it's a political event to try and force change and create a better, more just society. We didn't really feel or see that place for black people within the mainstream Pride events, so we said, "Right, what are we going to do about this?" There was no point in moaning and saying, "Oh look, the white people who run Pride aren't making it nice for us." So we said, "OK, let's try and create a space of our own".'

But over the last 10/11 years, the pain I have felt at being rejected by the wider, mainly white gay LGBT+ community, who didn't and don't see their privilege whilst blocking Black Pride for wanting to be visible, is not something I can bear to explain. But I'm sure as you are reading this *Sista!* anthology – you get it; you see I have carried this and tried to shield our communities and fight tooth and nail against those who don't see that racism is a weapon of mass destruction. Even some parts of the Black/BME/PoC LGBTQI+ community have not been as welcoming or supportive as I would have hoped, but I try to look at the root causes of why we have been a little fragile, fragmented and traumatised. We are not just battling with surviving being black, but with the many different parts of where our lives intersect with each other – like being a black woman who identifies as a disabled woman of faith who deals with class issues – I could go on!

It's almost laughable that activists who have been part of a liberation struggle in which we as LGBT people had to fight to be seen, heard and allowed to take pride in our place in society – a fight we still have to fight today; activists who also declare loudly that they are a community that understands oppression and marginalization – do not wish to support the struggle and adverse challenges LGBT People of Colour face. It felt and feels like sheer, messed up hypocrisy. Just because you are from a group that has been discriminated against, it doesn't exempt you from being racist, sexist, biphobic, transphobic, disablist, ageist and then some – please check yourself!

I've always said, 'In an ideal world we would not need a Pride; in an ideal world we certainly would not need a Black Pride. However, we do not live in an ideal world, and whilst we find ourselves being tortured, persecuted, criminalised or even murdered because of our sexual orientation, non-conforming gender-identity, or because of the colour of our skin, our ethnicity, our HIV status, religious belief, our class and refugee or asylum status – UK Black Pride will continue challenging and working from within and outside with community grass-roots campaigners, trade unions, and organisations such as Stonewall, UKLGIG (UK Lesbian & Gay Immigration Group) among others.'

I am the way I am. I joke about 'weave and nails', and those who do not know me think I'm a black Barbie, but my efforts have been recognised with a nomination for an MBE – Medal of the Most Excellent Order of the British Empire. But this is how serious I am about equality, equity, social justice and freedom: I had to reject without hesitation the Queen's honour because, 'I don't believe in the empire. I don't believe in, and actively resist, colonialism and its toxic and enduring legacy in the Commonwealth, where – among many other injustices – LGBTQI+ people are still being persecuted, tortured and even killed because of sodomy laws that still exist' – laws put in place by British imperialists.

So the blogs and nasty, hateful Twitter posts by trolls and keyboard warriors can hurt, but my personal plea to you, our communities, is that if you truly call yourselves progressives and wish to see intersectionality take pride of place in all that we do, please do not stay silent: show solidarity, be a good ally and not a bystander.

Now the UK Black Pride event attracts support from around the world and a wide cross-section of society, including Members of Parliament, trade unions, Black and LGBT community and voluntary groups, providers of public services such as the police and primary care trusts, as well as young people and students. Most importantly though, UK Black Pride continues to be supported by the community it serves, to ensure the principle of 'Pride before Profit', and to guarantee that UK Black Pride remains an inclusive event for all in our community.

I believe that, with the right approach to supporting Prides as I have done over the years – I helped set up and advise on the first Paris Black Pride in 2016 – there is a formula that can work for all of us; for activists and the community where we meet the corporate brands. UK Black Pride's approach has been effective. We will only source from ethical companies, and I hope that I have constantly reinforced the message that Pride came from the Stonewall riots, and that it is important to claim spaces that are otherwise closed to us. We must never forget the protest element to Pride or allow it to be sidelined. UK Black Pride is always about ensuring the sponsorship we have goes back into building our communities. And we ensure that there is a strong message of equality and justice which underpins the very reason we exist.

This is a strong social message, and is at the heart of what we do. This is what makes me proud to be the Co-Founder and Executive Director of UK Black Pride.

If you want to get involved, visit the UK Black Pride website www.ukblackpride.org.uk; tweet @ukblackpride or join the UK Black Pride Facebook page.

I leave you with a quote from an iconic inspirational figure, Audre Lorde:

'I write for those women who do not speak, for those who do not have a voice because they were so terrified, because we are taught to respect fear more than ourselves. We've been taught that silence would save us, but it won't. So in our work and in our living, we must recognize that difference is a reason for celebration and growth, rather than a reason for destruction.'

Solidarity #BlackFistSalute

babirye bukilwa: 4 poems

Lungs

Every time my heart stops
self hating and becomes the organ it's meant to fucking be I
form a new pattern.
Sing a new song. The love I have for her
will never be the same love I have for her.
Why does it need to be?
If it was I wouldn't want it. I'm okay with my many criss cross
heart
melting into water
forming black ice into souls
Sometimes the thickness of the thread makes it difficult
to get through the whole
Of me
Whilst my heart is a rainbow scarf of threads and strings and
colour,
Whilst my heart is an emerging ocean, overwhelming coastlines
Whilst my heart is an open
My eyes are closed
And I allow you to pour concrete
Into
My lungs

Nalongo (mother of twins)

I have to remind myself that you are here and never left.
that the essence of you kisses the insides of my belly. Not your
face.
What is 'leave'?
How long is 'leave' if you are just away. For a while.
You are in the next room.
Your smell still exists. I can smell you
I feel you
gold

Morning

Oh morning
Old foe.
Old lover.
What is it about you?
Your smell, your walk.
I've danced with you many times.
Nobody moves the way you move
 I know your whine. I know that ass.
We used to make love with
Stamina. hypnotic rhythm.
What is it about you.
You never tire.
I used to hate you.
Fear u.
A constant reminder of my tears
that weren't caught in a tissue.
like somebody poking a bruise on my side.
like I was being gassed
Your wicked unnerving, unforgiving whine.
Sometimes that slow
Tick tock
the glare of your stare
Through a window would floor me.
You were too real.
invasive
Sometimes the smell of your cum choked me to death
I wasn't ready to transform
Waking up sober with you was painful
I forced you out of my room
Of my lungs
I married your brother
I fucked your sister
It wasn't as good. It never was
What is it about you

Morning

Then I danced with your mum one time.

One whine
Is all it took. She caught me off guard and held my hips. Kissed
my temples and took it slow
For me to catch my breath.
I caught a two step.
She told me I am the morning. That I
was always
The morning.

Pour

I'll bring you flowers in the pouring rain
I'll go therapy, so I'm no longer insane
I'll bring you flowers, they'll make your day
I'll go therapy – no longer in your way
Because you feel like Coltrane
And Sade
And you know what: I'm dramatic and corny and super intense,
but see I can still rhyme, and be funny, and take your favourite
songs, and change them a bit, or make them sillier or shitter,
and then when you hear the shit original you'll think of me.
Us, me.
Me.
And I'll stop over thinking
and over analysing
and over complicating
and over complicating
and over complicating already complicated issues because you
don't like how anxious I get because it makes you anxious.
And I'll stop not taking off my make up before bed because
whilst MAC is affordable it comes off like a mother fucker and
you like white bed sheets.
And I'll stop wearing my outside clothes on your inside bed,
and change into my inside clothes because I'm getting into bed
with you.
And I'll take more breaths when I speak
And I'll stop singing around the house, I'll even stop singing
hello to you and stop trying to find the harmonies to make
them sound prettier for when I sing them to you.
And I can stop saying I love you so much.
And I'll make your tea just right all the time
Not just when I want you to fuck me harder or slower or just
fuck at all
And I've stopped saying FUCK IT to everything and everyone
because when you sprinkle too much FUCK IT among things

that need exactitude and care you become fucked
Indefinitely.
I can stop saying I love you so much
I can stop offering you physical spliffs when you tell me you're
sad and roll you mental ones instead?
I can stop saying I love you so much?
That will be hard
I still cry for no reason.
Beautiful girl
Sorry; woman
Sorry; person
Beautiful creature in my veins, I can love you less, I can take
more breaths when I speak, I can love you different,
I can even love you in slow motion
I won't drown in you anymore – I'm not thirsty
See the boat was holed from the beginning and I used my
eyeballs to stop the leak and split my heart in two so I could see
And because the water was boiling
Everybody told me it was hot
And because the water was boiling
Everybody told me it was hot
And because the water was boiling my throat is now a passage
of burnt flesh, so I'm not really thirsty anymore.
I want to bring you to a crescendo
I think kissing you again would be an adventure
I still cry for no reason
Mans is still here
You made so much sense
 You make no sense at all
 When sea otters sleep they hold their lover's hand
I think I am an orangutan
What is freedom?
I realised I perform my gender
What is freedom?
I realised I perform my gender
I want to roll you zoots

Why did I give her to you?
All I wanted to do was bring you freedom because apparently
it's the shit
But for now, will flowers do?

Christina Fonthes

After my 27th birthday my life changed. My name was plastered all over the news: 'Lesbian Activist Held Captive'. Petitions were signed. Queer and straight folk gathered in my name. My mother had taken me back 'home' to Congo. Having a lesbian daughter was too much for her to handle: it was unAfrican.

Two years after the 'incident' I reached out to my mother. 'Home Again' is a monologue I wrote about this experience. It was first performed at the Commonword Black and Asian Writers Conference, and at the Black Gold Arts Festival in 2016 as a supporting act for poet Lemn Sissay.

Home Again

Setting: character is at a bus stop talking to her best friend – audience is the friend.

So, I went to see her for the first time in two years. The other day.
Went to London.
I had to get the coach – cos you know – Richard Branson won't let me take the train. So I had to get on this super-packed coach to London.
I got on the Megabus, and it was the usual, like, massive delays Ten million people tryna get on.
It was literally like the Africa Express!
Like, all of these families *(laughs)* tryna move themselves – I swear some of these people actually use the coach to move houses.
You see people, like, carrying the weirdest stuff with them – saw someone with a lampshade. And this woman with like three kids and all these Ghana Must Go bags – is that term not PC? Am I allowed to say that? Well, *laundry bags* then. And I'm just thinking, where on earth are you going?
So, yeah, got on the coach and the journey was super long,

super sweaty. It was raining up until we left Manchester – of course!

And we had one of those coach drivers who was really arsy about everything.

So, somebody brought on some food – some hot food, which you're apparently not allowed to bring onto the coach, and he was like threatening to stop at the motorway.

He kept on making these announcements like 'Put the food away or I'll have to stop at the hard shoulder' and, 'It's illegal to bring hot food onto the vehicle.' And, I'm there just thinking – just drive the bloody bus Inspector Morse.

It was really hot and sweaty and nasty. You know there's that really nasty coach smell? It's like a mixture of like people's regrets *(laughs)* and really strong body odour, and you know, people's food from the previous evening, and it all just like sticks to you. It's so horrible.

Obviously I needed to pee cos I had that urinary infection, and the toilet wasn't working, so I'm on the coach for like six hours with a toilet that doesn't work but stinks like a portaloo at a festival, and this bus driver thinks he's some sort of commander-in-chief about to bring down the Iranian government!

(deep sigh)

But anyway, we got there in the end, and obviously we hit London and there's traffic like, everywhere. We were at a standstill for about an hour. It was just crazy.

(laughs)

The whole journey down there was crazy. The person next to me was on the phone the whole time – I still can't do the mean girl face to stop people sitting next to me. I've tried – doesn't work. So they're on the phone the whole journey and I'm just thinking, 'God please let me get off this coach,' and on the other hand I'm like, 'God please don't let this journey end', cos then it means I'll actually have to get off the coach and do what I gotta do. But got there in the end – in one piece.

Thank Goodness.

(deep sigh)

And yeah, made my way to the house. Got on the bus, and I was there.

And, it was strange.

It was – it was like one of those really surreal experiences where everything is exactly the same but somehow things are different, you know?

So, all of the shops were still there. Well, some of the shops were there – some of them had gone. Cos you know, gentrification and all of that stuff. The old internet café that was owned by the Somali guy was no longer there. It was now some sort of shisha place, which was really weird for that area cos there's usually, like, muggings and stabbings and that kind of stuff – and now it's like shisha. Here? Really?

(long sigh)

But hey, that's the world we live in now.

I was shitting myself. I really was. It'd been two years since we'd even spoken. Since we'd even said 'hello' to each other on the phone. And, I had no idea what to expect.

I was… literally shaking. I was sweating – from the coach. But also just from, you know, being nervous. And thinking, is it going to be okay? Like, is she gonna let me in? Is she gonna see me, is she gonna… *(nervous laugh)* you know, cuss me out? What's gonna happen? I mean, two years is a very long time in someone's life. Think about the amount of… you know… growth that a child has from 2 to 4 or 4 to 6. There's a lot that happens in that time. So, obviously, I was really nervous.

But I went, and… Yeah. I knocked on the door – well I pressed the buzzer, and the door just opened. She didn't say anything – she just let me in.

I went upstairs - and even like walking up the stairs – again, it was like memory lane. There were the cigarette butts on the floor from the teenage boys that were smoking, you know, behind their parents' backs and stuff.

It's three flights of stairs – I was so out of breath by the time I got to the top – I was like shit I really need to stop smoking *(laughs)* but yeah, obviously, I've not stopped.

So, yeah went up the stairs, got there. The door was open, and I kinda just stood there for about two seconds before I went in just sort of like, you know prepping myself, like, 'You're gonna be okay, you're gonna be okay, you've got this, it's fine, it's fine. You can do this.'

And she was there.

And it was crazy. It was so many feelings and emotions that I'd been tryna suppress. You know.

I think James Baldwin says something like, the reason that people don't let go of their anger is because they're afraid of the pain they'll feel once the anger's gone.

And I think that's very true. I was so scared of feeling anything but anger. Cos anger's a strange thing like that isn't it? Like, it can actually keep you going. It's a really negative emotion but sometimes, it kinda fuels you. And I really felt like the anger it just went. It just dropped the moment I saw her. It just completely fizzled out. And all these other feelings came through that I'd been suppressing.

Like the missing. You know?

I really, really, fucking missed her.

And she missed me too.

I could see it in her face. And looking at her was like looking at myself. But not myself. I know that sounds a bit weird – like it's me but it's not me. Cos we look alike, a lot.

And, it's again that whole thing of time had gone but it hadn't gone.

So she'd aged obviously, cos it'd been two years. But she also looked, really, like a child.

You know, there was a sort of nervousness that she had that I recognised straight away because I felt it too. And she held me. Really, really tight. Like to the point where I kind of like, jumped back.

(laughs)

And that's not the norm for us because we don't usually kiss, and touch, and hold each other, and hug, you know. Except if it's something dramatic like somebody's died, and then you can cry as much as you want, you can hold on to people and you can hug people, and you can squeeze 'em. But other than that it's generally weird to just hug someone.

I mean we were colonized by the French and Belgians so we usually greet each other with kisses on the cheeks.

But, we held each other really, really tight.

And I almost dropped.

You know.

And it was good.

It was good.
You know.
Time had passed. And everything that had happened,
everything she'd said,
everything I'd said.
It kinda just fizzled.
We needed that time apart.
We really needed that time apart to think about each other.
And to miss each other.
And that's what happened.
We hugged and she kissed me.
She said she was sorry about Orlando – the shootings. That was
her apology.

And before I went she said 'ba tika ka mama te' –
I'll always be your mother.

(fade to black)

*

After Congo, I sought solace in writing poetry. The counselling,
the meds – all were helpful, but through poetry I could explore
the unnameable feelings. Through writing poetry, I found I
needed to forgive. I wrote 'Ruth and Naomi' after a conversation about religion and sexuality.

Ruth and Naomi

*Where you go I will go, and where you stay I will stay. Your
people will be my people and your God my God. Where you
die, I will die, and there I will be buried. Thus may the LORD
do to me, and worse, if anything but death parts you and me.*

Ruth 1: 1-17

Forgive the pentecostal pastor
who preaches five hour sermons
on the dangers of our tongues – sins

Forgive the mother, the father

whose knees have blackened lamenting
they have taken matters into their own hands – gods

Forgive the sisters
who hope we will change
'you've spent too much time away from home' – bounty

Forgive the aunts
who accept us but not our ways
a prayer of thanks their own daughters will bear children
– blessings

Forgive the state
for forgetting 200 stolen girls
whilst signing the lynchings of men old enough to marry
– blood

Forgive the five men
who cornered us in the night
gleaming teeth and fire in their eyes – hell

Forgive the judges
in that courtroom who made us show them
how we spread our legs, only to say 'no' – destitute

Forgive us for believing
Heaven is reserved for women
who love men – faith

Andreena Bogle-Walton: 4 poems

INNER VOICE

There was a voice inside waiting to be heard
Inner thoughts and feelings far from absurd
Holding back the tears for so many years
Due to negative judgement and fears
Fear of being rejected
Fear of being isolated
Fear of being violated
Fear from people with unrelenting hatred
Fear of feeling that if i stayed confined i would eventually lose
my mind
Buried deep inside
There was nowhere left to hide
That inner voice needed to come out
Needed to bellow and shout
Because i too am worthy in all my human glory.

I AM FREE

I came out as a lesbian in 2003
All the clues were there it's just that i couldn't see
People knew i was gay before me
Or is it that i didn't want to see and be true to me?
People were too judgemental back then
In the '90s and way back when
I'm gonna take a bow
Cos i'm happy now
I am free to finally be who i'm meant to be
Loving living this reality within the LGBTIQ+ community
My family may not be proud of me but i'm able to maintain my
sanity and not let them get the better of me mentally
Live and let live i say cos every dog has its day
Life is for living come what may.

50 SHADES OF GREEN

There's 50 shades of green on the lesbian scene
But there's only one you should be keeping keen
Don't look over the fence to find 50 pence because she's the only one that should make sense
You can have your cake and eat it too cos you can share it between the two of you
Don't go looking over the hedge to plant your seed in her vegetable patch
You already have the perfect catch
Other girls will be on her ass
But you just need to keep her well within your grasp
Not to be the controlling type but to be the only one she likes
There's always gonna be 50 shades of green
You just need to keep your eyes open on the lesbian scene.

JUST US

When i breathe the air i breathe you breathe it with me
And i beg you not to leave
It's just us
When after the rain comes a thunder storm
It's not you it's me that keeps us safe and warm
Don't ring the alarm and pull the plug
Hold me close and give me a hug
It's just us
Trust
This relationship could easily crumble into dust
This is because we are existing without lust
It's been you and me for months
It's just us
I need you to believe in me and wait for me to deal with the
things that are plaguing me
I need you to see that this is real but not our reality
Not based on vanity but based purely on love and loyalty
Just give me some time to bring back the sunshine in my smile
I promise you it will be worth your while.

Lettie Precious

On The Job

Talia was frustrated with her life. She'd never left London, she was broke, unemployed and depressed. She punched and kicked the boxing bag in a frenzy until Terry, the gym's manager, intervened.

'Slow down, kid, I won't have no equipment left the way you're going at it.'

Stopping, sweat trickling down her mahogany skin. 'Sorry Terry, it's just one of those days.'

Terry was a big, intimidating skinheaded white man with a cockney accent and faded tattoos. To complete his look, he rode a heavy-duty 'Super Low' silver Harley. He had built quite a reputation in South East London in his prime. Having done hard time in Wandsworth Prison, rumour had it that Terry had run the place and even the screws had been terrified of him. But when a ten-year-old black girl from the children's orphanage walked into his gym thirteen years ago, she had melted his heart. Now, looking at the young woman before him, he wanted to take away her sadness. 'What is it, kid? If there's anyfink I can do.'

She knew he was only trying to look out for her. She'd often find a small envelope of money in her locker at the end of the month, but she always returned it. It hurt him, but Talia was too proud to take hand-outs. Feeling sorry for herself, and Terry's old, smelly gym reminding her of how stagnant her life was, a decision was made: for once in her life she was going to take charge of her destiny and get what was hers.

'Thanks Terry, I appreciate it but I've got go. I'll see you next week, okay?'

Not waiting for him to respond, she left his gym, leaving a bereft Terry watching his little girl walk away with the weight of the world on her shoulders.

The day had finally come. She had been planning this for weeks now. Every detail had been laid out meticulously. After today money wouldn't be an issue. She'd finally have peace of mind. Talia mounted her bicycle and set off to Brixton. She was dressed all in black and wore a backpack. It was the weekend and the market stalls were bustling. Her stomach rumbled when she pedalled past the Caribbean stands, the rich aromas taunting her nostrils. A man stood on the kerb about to bite into his jerk chicken and she snatched it from his hand and sped away. 'What the bomba-clart!' The insults faded the further she went. Parking her bike round the corner, Talia sat on the pavement and devoured the meat. As she ate, she prepared her mind to face what was to come.

She wiped her hands on the back of her jeans and resumed her journey, cycling over to Chelsea. She'd marked three homes, noted their routines, and worked out how to disarm their alarm systems, thanks to a few online tutorials. She quickly donned on a Royal Mail jacket she had bought online and carried a parcel.

After ringing the front doorbell of her first target repeatedly to make sure no-one was in, she made her way down the side-passage to the rear of the house. Pulling on a ski-mask she stretched up on tiptoe to spray-paint the lenses of the CCTV cameras that watched the patio doors, with a can from her backpack. Time was of the essence: she had only ten minutes to do the job and leave.

The first two houses were easy enough. Rich people were so careless about their belongings, she mused, as she stuffed ornaments and other knickknacks into her backpack. Instead of feeling bad, she felt good about taking some of their wealth. Why should people like her suffer and these people live like royalty? She was just balancing things out and making right with the universe.

Heading to the final house, she was elated. Her task was almost over and adrenalin pumped at the thought of having pulled it off. Upon approaching the large, detached Edwardian dwelling, Talia noticed something peculiar about the setting presented before her. The light on the alarm was off, and the front door was slightly ajar. Her sense told her to leave, but greed and curiosity won. She slowly snuck in, careful to not make any sound.

Talia cringed when the mahogany stairs creaked under her feet as she made her way up to the first floor. She came to a long, dimly lit corridor and pondered which direction to take. She opted to go right, hoping it would lead her to the master bedroom. She crept along the wall and listened for movement. As she entered what looked like the main suite she sensed a movement from behind the door and ducked instinctively – her black belt in martial arts had gotten her out of many sticky situations in the past.

A fist came flying towards her face and she yelped, blocking it. Jumping up, Talia jabbed two fingers in her assailant's throat and kneed him hard in the crotch. The man dropped to floor, grabbing at his testicles, groaning in pain.

'Oh...Ah...Bloody hell! You broke my nuts you dim cow!'

She was surprised by his accent – 'a posh thief, how interesting,' she thought to herself. When upright the man had towered over her five foot nine frame. She guessed he was a little over six feet tall. Judging by his athletic physique and speed she was sure he was in his late twenties or early thirties, although she would have to remove his mask to be sure. Chest heaving, she retorted, 'That's what you get for trying to punch me in the face!'

'I'm protecting my territory,' he snarled, struggling to his feet. Tugging off her mask, which was making it hard to breathe, Talia watched him carefully, ready for anything. Sensing her wariness, he grumbled, 'Calm down, will you; I won't try anything, that kick to the balls is enough for today, thank you very much.'

As the pain receded the man appraised the woman before him, curious eyes roaming over her flawless, sun-kissed skin, her athletic but feminine physique. Her perfectly symmetrical face, blessed with thick lips and framed by a thick Afro, most impressed him.

A clearing of the delicate throat brought him back to reality. 'When you're quite done ogling me, we need to decide how we're going to play this out. I marked this house too, and I think it's only fair to split the loot.'

'No chance! This is my turf and you're trespassing. You

aren't getting sh...'

She didn't let him finish his sentence. Putting her hand over his mouth, she whispered, 'I think there's someone downstairs, let's grab what we can and leave.'

But footsteps were already clumping up the stairs.

Now they were approaching the bedroom.

Desperate to find a hiding place, Talia climbed up on top of a large wardrobe and pressed herself out of sight against the wall whilst the man squeezed himself under the bed. Talia's heart nearly stopped when she peeped down and saw a police-man looking around. He wore a bulletproof vest. Pulling out a gun, the officer said quietly into his radio, 'Sarge, we have a BIP, possibly still in progress. I'm checking the area now.'

He bent down to look under the bed, and was surprised by a kick to the face. He stumbled backwards, hitting his head on the dresser behind him, and passed out with a grunt. Talia swung down from the wardrobe and her co-conspirator emerged from under the bed.

The officer's radio boomed in the silence, startling them both. 'What's your status, Jack? Back up is on its way. Jack? ...Respond Jack! I'm coming up.... Attention all units we have a code red, code red!'

Frantically looking for an escape route, they were faced with two doors. The first one they yanked open was a walk-in wardrobe, the second, a small bathroom. Running into it, they found its single window high up and sealed shut. The man searched in the bag he carried and whipped out a chisel. One sharp act of levering did the job. Before he could do anything more, Talia clambered up his back onto his shoulders. She climbed out onto the flat roof of a rear extension, turned and pulled him up after her. He was heavy and almost fell back, but by bracing her feet against the wall she managed to counterbal-ance him.

Sirens blared in the distance, drawing near. The pair wasted no time jumping over the fence into the next-door garden, but found a pit-bull waiting for them. It was chained, but the chain was the length of the garden. 'Calm down little shit,' Talia tried as it came towards them snarling and slavering, but the man tasered the dog before it could attack.

'What the hell's wrong with you?' Talia said, looking down

at the twitching dog now lying on its back and foaming at the mouth.

He shrugged. 'At least I didn't call him a little shit. We've got no time for this, my car's parked down the block if you want a ride.'

She hesitated. 'My bike's behind the house, they'll find it.'

'You can just say it got nicked. Get a move on.'

Ducking into a nearby garden they changed into different clothes – thank god Talia had thought of that as part of her escape plan. The man put on a nicely tailored shirt and, parting and sleeking his hair to the side, he looked very respectable. Talia donned a nice blouse and 'professional' brown wig. Now they looked like they belonged.

The pair made an unhurried exit through the front gate and watched the commotion unfold as the police hunted about for the thieves. The man slipped his arm around Talia's waist and she nestled into his shoulder. Like a doting mother, she cradled the loot she had wrapped in a cloth like a baby. As they passed an officer guarding the crime scene, Talia's new partner in crime turned to him. 'Everything alright? I live a couple of houses along and obviously I'm worried about Ruth and John.' The policeman naively answered his question after inquiring if the man had seen anything suspicious. 'I wish I could help you, but my wife and I literally just got in and' – indicating Talia's cradled swag – 'are now on our way to the doctor with our son, mandatory check-up.'

The policeman apologised for keeping them and they went on. Talia dared to look back and saw the officer from upstairs being lifted unconscious into an ambulance on a stretcher, a distressed black woman in a sergeant's uniform by his side. The woman looked up then and their eyes locked. Time seemed to stop for Talia until her new partner grabbed her arm.

'You'll give us away,' he said through gritted teeth, pulling her forward. 'Amateur.'

She threw an annoyed look at him although she knew he was right. 'What's your name anyway?' she asked as they turned the corner. 'Our son deserves to know his father's name,' she added, looking at their makeshift baby.

'Beautiful and a sense of humour... I'm Gordon,' he smirked.

'Typical white boy name,' she joked. She told him her name as they got in his red Dutson 240Z and drove away. Talia was enthralled by the beauty of his car – the bold thrust of its bonnet; the effortless acceleration – and imagined she'd be owning something that spectacular soon.

She could tell Gordon was from 'old money'. He had the arrogance of a spoilt brat but had a charming quality to him too. Talia appreciated a good-looking man when she saw one. Without his mask Gordon was handsome, with good bone structure and chiselled features. His brown hair was thick and artfully messy and his deep blue eyes a direct contrast to her light brown ones. She wondered why he was doing what he did. Did he really need the money? Perhaps he did, but his sense of entitlement made him too proud to get a regular job. She was too proud too, but his motives weren't really her concern. What she needed was someone more experienced in the art of theft than she was.

They agreed to split the loot: Talia had better connections in Brixton to move stolen gear. She made two thousand pounds that day and her fate was sealed. This was her new hustle.

After that day, she decided to form a business partnership with Gordon. Her gamble was proving to be a very lucrative venture. In the past month there had been a new addition to the team, Fatimah. She had approached Talia in what seemed to be a random encounter at a café, then claimed to know about her criminal activities. Fearing blackmail or worse, Talia had at first angrily denied it, but became intrigued when the woman expressed interest in joining her team. Her exact words were, 'I know I'm a Muslim girl and I should be a doctor or something but all that's boring. I'm an IT genius and I can make you rich.'

'What's in it for you?'

'Life!' she simply replied.

Talia had been sceptical, but when she made her first ten thousand pounds from a job initiated by Fatimah, she welcomed her with open arms. The only condition Fatimah had was that they take specifically from bad and corrupt people. Gordon was on board with the new member and the new areas they could explore with Fatimah's skills. Talia understood him better by then: he was always chasing the thrill: the bigger the risk, the better the rush.

Their next mark was Romano Santino, one of the biggest sex-traffickers in London. Taking him on was dangerous, but would mean a big payday for all of them.

'What will you do with the money?' Talia asked Fatimah as they sat about chatting in Gordon's warehouse flat.

'Pay my student debt,' she shrugged.

With his mouth full of popcorn, Gordon put in his two cents. 'I owe some very bad men big bucks in Vegas.'

'You need our help dealing with them?'

Gordon eyed her. 'Where's the fun in that? No, I'm a big boy, I can handle it, but come a time I need my gal pals, I shall summon thee. Now, we need to work out how we're going to pull this rabbit out of the hat.' The plan was to infiltrate Santino's organisation by whatever means necessary.

Gordon and Fatimah stayed in the nondescript white van while Talia went into the club. They watched her through their surveillance camera. As the doors swung shut behind her, the smoky, intimate atmosphere hit her and her stomach lurched. She descended a winding staircase, seductively floating to the sultry music coming from the basement. The steel-shod spiky heels of her patent-leather boots clinked, drawing eyes. When she opened and then removed her black leather trench-coat, mouths opened moistly. She wore a tight black leather mini-skirt and a black see-through bikini top that showed off her toned midriff and barely covered her perky breasts. The shiny leather boots came up to the tops of her thighs, and her unapologetic Afro completed her Blaxploitation hooker look.

The patrons, all of whom seemed to be female, wore masquerade masks. Talia touched her earpiece. 'Do you see the mark?' David's voice vibrated in her cochlea. He'd been annoyed that he couldn't do the job himself because it was women's night. He was dying to see the show.

'Not yet,' she murmured as a burlesque dancer took the stage. Captivated, she watched the woman start to seduce the audience. 'Her, she's perfect.'

The woman was beautiful and would certainly make getting information fun. She was slender but curvaceous in the right places. Her caramel skin glowed against the matte blackness of her corset. Languidly she scoped the room. She saw Talia. Their eyes locked. Slowly she made her way across to where Talia stood. Talia had the strangest feeling of deja vu. She thought she saw a fleeting recognition in the woman's eyes too, but a seductive smokiness quickly replaced it.

Pressing her breasts into Talia's chest, the woman whispered in her ear with a sultry Scottish accent, 'You're new here.' It wasn't a question but a statement. When Talia didn't respond, the woman turned her head slightly and kissed Talia on the cheek, then the lips. Heat spread through Talia's body and her pupils dilated. This job was getting better by the second. The woman flushed. Moaning she deepened the kiss, demanding to explore Talia's mouth. Talia welcomed the warmth and the velvety feel of the woman's tongue. The crowd's cheers and whistles reminded them where they were. Wondering if this had all been a show, Talia heard Gordon's wolf-whistle through her earpiece followed by a grunt, and guessed Fatimah had elbowed him. The dancer swayed her way back to the stage.

She waited for the burlesque dancer to finish her set and slipped backstage after her, following her down a dimly lit corridor, noting cameras and avoiding all surveillance spots. At its far end was a door through which the dancer vanished. As Talia neared it she bumped into a burly black man she suspected was one of Santino's goons, buttoning his fly as he came out of the adjacent toilet. She tried to control her pounding heart and fumbled for words. Mistaking her for one of the performers, he smiled and let her go by. Relieved, Talia followed the other woman through the door into a small office with dirty, grilled windows, and caught the burlesque dancer rummaging through cabinets. When the dancer realised she had an audience, she seemed to panic. 'What are you doing in here?' she asked sharply. Then, attempting a smile: 'You startled me.'

Talia smiled too. 'I thought we had unfinished business. Did you lose something?'

'No, I'm looking for the boss's stash. The best scotch in town he calls it.'

Talia noticed slight perspiration forming on the woman's forehead. 'Do you want me to help you look? I'm good with my hands,' she said with a cheeky grin.

'I bet you are. On second thoughts,' the dancer said, crossing to the door, 'let's go to the bar. Drinks are on me.' She seemed anxious to leave the room but Talia didn't question it; her plan was coming together perfectly.

They flirted as they drank straight spirits, and by their tenth jaeger bomb they were kissing passionately. The woman's eyes were glazed with fiery desire. Standing between Talia's legs, she ran her tongue along her jawline to her ear and whispered, 'Take me to bed now!'

Talia shivered when the seductress took her earlobe in her mouth and sucked on it.

She woke up when a soft hand smacked her limply in the face. It took her a minute to realise she was back in her apartment and the extra limbs weren't hers. Her head pounded and she felt nauseous. Her body was both sore and humming from the aftermath of great sex. Turning her head, she traced the woman's face with her eyes. The memories of the night before came flooding back as the woman's eyes fluttered open and she smiled, exposing the dimples in her cheeks. Talia's heart skipped. How gorgeous this woman was! Her light cocoa skin was fanned with freckles, and long eyelashes guarded her hazel eyes. Her hair was straight but Talia could tell that if water came anywhere near it the curls would be fierce.

She struggled to remember the woman's name, and started to feel extremely awkward. She had never brought a one-night stand home before. If the woman sensed her discomfort, she didn't show it. She pulled Talia in for a smouldering kiss. Instantly all anxiety left Talia's body, and the heat between her legs took charge.

A while later they lay breathless staring at the ceiling, their rumbling bellies announcing hunger pangs. The woman finally broke the silence: 'What's your name?' She hid under the duvet in shame.

Talia laughed and peeked through the covers. 'Would it calm you down if I told you I don't remember yours either?'

They both laughed. 'Rae, Rachel... I'm Rachel Simmons.' She extended her hand to Talia.

'I'm Sam,' Talia said, using her middle name. 'You're a great dancer, Simmons.' Rachel smiled at the compliment. Still aware of the task at hand, Talia needed to dig deeper to extract useful intel on Romano Santino. 'How long have you been working at the club?' She watched the woman closely.

'Not that long, three months. Do you make a habit of picking up women at sex clubs?' she teased.

'Maybe... What's it like working there?'

She shrugged. 'It is what it is. Why, do you need a job?'

'Maybe... and if I do, I'd want someone to look out for me... help me get to know the place before I sell my soul.'

Rachel looked at her as if she was trying to solve a puzzle, then reached for her hand and kissed it. 'How about I make us some brunch?' She walked over to Talia's fridge, opened it, frowned. 'You need to do some shopping.' She continued to look through the kitchen cupboards carrying low expectations. 'Voila! I've managed to find one mouldy plantain and a couple of years-old ackee and saltfish, brilliant! I'll make you a proper Caribbean brunch.'

Talia laughed. 'How about you're the longest one-night stand ever,' she teased.

'Oh you think this is a one-night stand do you? Did you not see the U-Haul truck parked outside? My mum's on her way.' Her face was so serious Talia almost believed her. Rachel burst out laughing. 'The look on your face is priceless. It's cute.'

Later that day Talia debriefed her team. They sat on Gordon's sofa and ate pizza. Of course he was the first to ask the lewd questions. 'How was the tongue and finger action?'

Fatimah smacked the back of his head.

'We used a strap-on actually,' Talia replied playfully.

'Why do lesbians do that, why not get the real thing?'

Fatimah and Talia looked at each other and rolled their eyes.

'Anyway, back to business: did you get any good intel?' Fatimah asked.

'Not yet, it's too early in the game. And there's something about her, I just can't put my finger on it'.

'Great choice of words', Gordon chimed in.

They moved on to other matters. They needed a legitimate way to move the large sums of money they were making without alerting the authorities. Eventually, Fatimah managed to create business accounts using dead children's records from hacked hospital files, setting up offshore accounts. 'Tax *avoidance*, not tax *evasion*,' Fatima said fastidiously. 'If only father could see me now! If you need me, I'll be off reading my Koran.' Fatimah was indeed an odd mix to the group, rebellious, well-intentioned with an air of mischief, but also the very much needed voice of reason.

During the meeting, they had all agreed that Rachel was the key to destroying Santino's sex trafficking organisation and making good money in the process. This was what Fatima called 'synergy'.

Talia was getting frustrated. She'd been seeing Rachel for two months now but the woman remained a closed book to her: though they enjoyed each other physically, both women kept emotional distance. However, the more time they spent together, making love and sharing common interests, the more the lines began to blur. Unexpectedly they discovered that they both loved adventure sports. Breaking away from the unhealthy, twilit world of the burlesque club they even took part in the annual Tough Mudder fitness obstacle course in Scotland.

They went rock climbing and hiking quite a few times and camped in Derbyshire's Peak District. Talia never let up on trying to penetrate Rachel's walls, but sometimes felt hers were being penetrated instead. If she were honest with herself, she would admit she was growing more deeply involved with Rachel with every passing moment, but denial and loyalty to her team kept her focused. She would sometimes go to watch Rachel's shows, and now had a better understanding of Santino's club and its routines.

This morning they'd gone to Terry's gym for a bit of sparring. Talia was teaching Rachel martial arts and was surprised at what a quick learner she was; it was as if she'd done it before, though Rachel insisted not.

They chatted as they punched and kicked at each other, vying for dominance. 'Do you realise you never really talk about your life? I still don't really know anything about you,' Talia said to Rachel whilst ducking a roundhouse kick.

'There's nothing to tell. I work, I go home, I see you and

that's that. Besides, you're not exactly forthcoming either,' she replied, blocking an uppercut from Talia.

'YOU... are deflecting... Let's do that last move again. When you block an uppercut always follow it up with a knee to the midsection, like this...' she demonstrated.

'I'm just a private person. Let's not complicate things, Sam.'

Talia raised her hands in surrender. 'Fine, whatever. I'm done for today, I'm going for a shower.' Her mood suddenly grim, she walked away before the other woman could respond. Rachel's words had hurt, and that wasn't good. She was getting attached and she didn't like it one bit. She pushed the feelings down and thought about the money she'd make from taking down Santino's club.

Today marked ten months of seeing Rachel, an anniversary of sorts, the longest relationship Talia had ever been in. In that time she had gathered enough information to pull off the biggest heist of her career. The team was going to steal, Fatima had estimated, over one million pounds of laundered money: Santino's club was a drop-off point for many illegal activities.

Though she had not let her colleagues know, today was also the day Talia was going to tell Rachel who she really was and how she really felt.

Hoping for a mutual response, she imagined them kissing passionately and skipping through flowery fields into the sunset with a heavy suitcase of cash.

After the job, the team agreed they would keep a low profile, because Santino and those he worked for would be looking for whoever robbed him.

The day they had been planning for had finally arrived. To pull it off, Talia had enlisted the help of the only other person she knew and could trust, Terry. With a weary shake of his head he'd grudgingly helped them source an unregistered black van with tinted windows and fake license plates. The van was equipped with surveillance feeds to the tiny cameras in the club that Talia had furtively placed over the course of her many visits, and the team parked it a street away from the building. Fatimah rigged the hacked club cameras through a wireless router to keep them showing the same shots of empty corridors. She then gave Talia a click detector to electronically manipulate and open the safe. Tensely wishing them luck, she watched Gordon and Talia cross to the building, pull on their masks, and creep in through a side door. Fatimah directed them, clearing their path.

'We found the safe,' she heard Talia say through the microphone.

'Good, now place the device on the safe door and key in the coordinates I gave you.'

She heard a beep then a click. 'Got it', Talia said.

They had a ten-minute window to pack the money into the individual backpacks they'd brought with them. 'The eagle has landed', Gordon said. Then, 'I've always wanted to say that.'

The packs filled, Fatimah began to navigate their escape route. 'Okay guys, if you go through the door on your right, there's a fire exit at the far end of the corridor... oh fudge cakes! You've got company.'

Before she could tell them more, her camera feed cut off and she heard gunshots through her earpiece. Working fast she scrambled to reconnect the server. When she managed to get back online she saw Gordon and Talia struggling with several heavyset men. What she didn't expect to see on the neighbouring screen was the Old Bill rushing into the building.

'Guys, you've got to get out of there now! The police are coming in.'

Keeping a keen eye on the surveillance feeds, Fatimah accessed the club's door-locking system and remotely locked the main door, stalling the police for a little while as they were forced to bust through. However, the face that appeared on Fatimah's screen stopped her dead in her tracks. 'Rachel!' The woman was now in police uniform and holding a gun. Clearly, they were working the place too, and had raced in when they heard the gunfire.

Fatimah switched the feed to find her team but they were gone. She watched the police pile into the office, only to find Santino's men out cold on the floor.

A bang on the van door startled her. She opened it to find Gordon and Talia standing there wide-eyed and panting, packs in each of their hands. Careful not to speed, they drove to Terry's lock-up. He was waiting for them. He helped them dispose of the van and hide the money.

Talia couldn't believe it. 'Show me the screenshot again.' She had been dumbstruck when Fatimah showed her the surveillance footage the day after the heist. Realising Rachel was Rebecca Hamilton, sergeant in the Metropolitan Police, was a bitter pill to swallow. How could she not have known? How could she have been so reckless? She was a professional thief for godsake. How could she have missed something she had mastered so well herself, the art of lying? The pieces were coming together now: the two phones, the private calls at all hours of the night. She remembered how she'd thought Rachel looked familiar that first night at the club. It was because she was the officer from the first job she'd ever done. She had been working undercover, and obviously Talia's team had implicated themselves into a major operation the night of the robbery. Thank god she hadn't followed through with telling Rachel – Rebecca – all about herself! She was still maintaining her cover unaware Talia had discovered her true identity. She'd been calling and texting her all week and had even come to Talia's flat a couple of times. Talia had ignored the buzzing of her intercom. Rachel had played the game very well. Talia was hurt and confused.

The immigration officer handed back her passport. 'Welcome to Spain.'

Talia stared at her mobile phone screensaver – her and Rachel's Tough Mudder picture beamed. There they were, standing under the pearly Scottish sky, covered in mud and wearing massive grins on their faces. With a sigh, she deleted it, closing that chapter. Sergeant Rebecca Hamilton was now a threat to her business. This changed everything...

P.J. Samuels: 3 pieces, 11 poems

Sometimes I cry because my dream does not wake with me

*

Some days I wrap my eyes around she sublime and I know this, women are God's apology. The way God said see, I can do something right...

*

And that was how she happened, a small whisper on a hurricane night

We slow danced neck to neck, cheek to cheek
You touched my hair
So beautiful you cooed
Is it yours
Huh?
I liked you, I mean I really liked you
Now why'd you have to come with some shit like that?

...Accordion

When they pull you apart
scream
Then pull yourself in and
make music...
Smile when they call it
black magic...
it is

BLACK SHE

Lather, rinse, repeat
I am black baby girl born
I am nappy hair
I am nigga pickney child
I am head tough
I am dark
I am old man's back pain
I am water scratch
I am isn't she beautiful though
I am salvation
I am prophesy
I am chance
I am bootstrap you pull yourself up by
I am melanin daughter, pretty for a black girl
I am pull and tug
I am war zone
I am trauma
I am do as you're told
I am sins and secrets
I am 4 a.m. broken
I am nervous tic
I am abdomen locked
I am tears on toilet
I am anxiety
I am body your fetish
I am body you sexualise
I am black girl dancing in white girl video
I am body you commodify
I am body too fat
I am body occupy too much space
I am body too dark
I am body cover it up
I am body take it off
I am body take it off now!
I am body for your gaze
I am body for your hands
I am body never my own
I am body never right

I am body black
I am body black and blue
I am body beaten
with your hands, your lips,
your lies, your whips
I am body contentious
I am body never simple
I am body for sex
I am sex on legs
I am sex in bed
I am sex on the counter top
I am sex bent over a chair
I am sex with boys
I am sex with girls
I am sex with girls who fuck like boys
I am sex with toys
I am naked picture on your wall
I am notch on your bedpost
I am symbol
I am a lady wouldn't do that though
I am get on with it
I am dinner ready
I am you're ugly
I am you're stupid
I am no-one else will want you
I am black eye at five
I am walk into doors
I am fall down stairs
I am broken hand
I am shattered femur
I am missing teeth
I am clumsy
I am accident
I am never again
I am I love you
I am you made me do this
I am apology and regret
I am take sleep and mark death
I am one hand wash the other
I am dialogue interrupted

I am silence
I am she asked for it
I am objectified
I am water under your bridge
I am stereotype
I am cliché
I am childbirth
I am messy things
I am stretchmarks
I am happiness deferred
I am sleepless nights, terrified
I am sing hallelujah and fingers crossed
I am fervent prayers
I am matriarch of black boys dead
I am coulda, woulda, shoulda
I am sorrow
I am bend and twist
I am stretch
I am fold in on myself
I am gripping belly pain
I am hymn at the funeral
I am soliloquy
I am in bed for 6 days
I am mental health intervention
I am pathology
I am prescriptions
I am self medicate
I am the joke that hung
around too long,
everyone had stopped
laughing
I am thank God I'm not her
I am shame
I am carry the weight of the world
I am meritocracy
I am token
I am put your back into it girl
I am guilt and apologies buried
I am elegy, platitudes
I am too little too late

I am graveyard
I am tomb
I am rest
I am woman
I am resurrection
I am woman
I am life
I am woman
I am damn marvellous
Lather rinse repeat
I am black baby girl born

REDEMPTION

All these things I'm meant to love because you told me to.
The callaloo that tastes like nothing.
Fish. School. The teachers. Church. The preachers. Correction.
It's meant to make me grow.
It really just destroys my confidence.
Laughter. Cats. Dogs. Donkeys.
Flowers, crotons in particular.
Roses have never been your thing.
You're a sucker for a pretty leaf.
Being handy.
Knowing where my food comes from, growing it.
My hair. You have always fiercely loved my hair.
You hated when I cut it off,
was bitterly disappointed when I straightened it.
You don't like dreads but you've told me my hair is beautiful.
I say thank you.
Quickly. I fear where the conversation could take us.
The boys. The girls. The men.
Because I should. You. Love.
I lick cashew seeds though their stain burns my lips and make
them sore.
Run my tongue over them.
I love the fruit.
I choke on tinkin toe as the dust congeals
in my throat and blocks my airway.
It's sweet.
I beat an almond pod with a stone for ages
trying to find the right angle to open it,
persist even when I miss and smash my fingers.
I love the seed inside.
And love is always worth it, right?
There is no too much I won't do and no so little I won't accept.
I love you.
I want to be you every day with my every breath.

I ate the compromises you lived and I have the strength they
nourished.
I am now older than you were when you fed me these things.
I farm at a supermarket counter.
I read the labels. Is that what redemption taste like?
I give too much.
My legs. My hairy skin.
You love these things, openly, loudly.
Bizzie tea.
It's meant to knock the poison out.
I don't think she loves me.
There is a chalk line marked around where I stand
and there's lead in the soles of my shoes.
You have always been proud of how strong I am.
It's a front verandah.
I lay all the muddy things there until the rain stops
and the sun shines through again.
Sometimes it storms in.
Sometimes it floods
everywhere.
Sometimes there is no shelter in strong.
No salvation.
Her every word is a prayer.
She says she loves me and I take anything.
Anything.
Like you, I have no idea what love means...

PARADOX

When we met you were bold
Full of bravado and affront
What you lacked in technique you made up for in confidence
And a beautiful willingness to be present
Present
Here
Now
Seeing
Me
When I stripped off your jaw dropped
When I touched you your breath caught in your throat
When I made you cum your scream started in your toenails
And I swear your tremors shook the sky
Between cold coffee and warm icecream we debated philosophy
When rights were wrong and doing wrong was right
We smiled
We kissed
Flirted with restraints and whips
You say you still love me...
So how come we not fucking anymore?

I moved into your house and it became our little dungeon
Reluctant to have friends over because the aura of us cumming
was seared into the walls
We used each inch of the house
Fucked so much letting anyone else sit on our couch was
sacrilege
Making it from the bath to the bedroom was running the
gauntlet
Taking a shower was foreplay
With handcuffs and nipple clamps we added pages to the Kama
Sutra
You say you still love me...
So how come we not fucking anymore?

Chocolate skin kept supple with cocoa butter
You said I'm the smoothest thing you ever seen
Beauty personified
Said having me made you feel like you touched a little piece of
heaven
And every time we fucked felt like the first time
Making you wanna celebrate
Roses and red wine were staples
Greek mythology over coffee in Starbucks
I ordered chocolate cake
You say you still love me...
So how come we not fucking anymore?

Lady Saw on the stereo
Ass bumping, I drop it like it's fire
Shaking it like my mama never taught me
You lick the sweat from my body
My fingers wrote memories on your skin
You said you loved the way my titties roll
The way my nipples come erect just from your smile
They still do
You kissing the back of my neck as I pen an ode to the curve of
your ass
Lust splashed on paper made real twixt bunched up cotton
sheets
Echoes in the unnatural arch of my spine
You say you still love me...
So how come we not fucking anymore?

You dressing to go out
I lie in bed watching you
Coffee skin glistens as you apply olive oil
Body parts bouncing around with your mindless self massage
Scents fill my nostrils and latent memories stir
They build unaided and my body screams for yours
But my lips stay silent

We've had that talk before
And my mind processed your words
Our tongues are battle axes
I'm battered
But I look at your body, and mine still makes that call
And yours still do not answer
And after all the intellectual discourse
I just still want to know
How come
How come
I want you to tell my aching crotch
If you really DO still love me
HOW COME WE NOT FUCKING ANYMORE?!!!

THE REASON

I did not sleep with you,
Understand this,
Is not that I did not fancy you.
I would not have written you
into my lifetime plans
anymore than you'd have written me into yours
but we'd have had a night.
There I was, indolent,
resplendent on your couch,
a body with no bones,
flesh held together with wanting you.
Replete on your food.
Inebriated on your jokes.
We took pictures.
Fiddled with the tv.
With each other.
You standing over me
You look so beautiful,
you said,
so slim and sexy.
Hold up, I said,
Sitting up,
how do those two things
connect in your mind?
Does sexy need to be slim?
Is slim always sexy?
No, no, no, you protested,
just you there, so beautiful.
My thoughts swirled around
untidy bodies and the chaos
of messy intertwinings.
I thought of what it would be like
to be peeling me off you.
I thought of my threshing reality

exploding all over
your beautiful myth.
I visualised the tornado of me
The full physical reality
of me coming.
So I decided I'd best let your fantasies,
curated and hosted by you,
reside uninterrupted
with you.

You are dance in impossible places
You are deliverance before anyone prayed
You are movement
You seamless segue from blues to jazz
You are music
You are fingers on life's guitar, baby strum
Let the unasked questions hang
Interrupting space like Christmas baubles
Let them spin
Cause you are answer
You are answer
You black magic miracle woman
You slay...
  ~ how can you not know?

REPENTANCE

Sit.
Sit with quiet.
Sit straight.
Breathe.
Pray.
Do not say her name.
Make patchwork quilt.
Drink coffee.
Recycle lies.
Avoid thinking.
Incinerate her letters.
Pray more.
Eve presented the apple. Do not bite.
Do not lick. Your lips.
She brings original sin.
Do not say her name.
Go to church. Take an umbrella.
It may rain.
Brimstone and fire.
Do not say her name.
Purify your thoughts.
'Oh God' is a shout of praise.
Do not blaspheme.
Bathe. In holy water.
Bake something. A tart.
Do not eat it.
Do not be it.
Stash memories in a jewellery box.
Polish them to a shine.
Do not paint your nails red.
Grow your hair.
Teach the bible how to beat.
Pray fervently, fundamentally.
Do not say her name.
Whatever happens, do not sin, no, never sin.
Feeling is not wanting is not needing.
If you throb for her, clean...
The carpet munching

on lemons.
Do not touch yourself when thoughts of her assault you.
Allow only the passion of Christ.
Clutch God fiercely between your legs.
Hide so well behind blind faith not even sleep can find you.
Do not say her name.
Prostrate.
Salvation is at the cross.
No, not bondage.
Talk to Jesus.
Rent your garments.
Cover yourself in ashes.
Chant beatitudes when abomination calls you friend.
Hallelujah is fifteen; you can only count to ten.
Burn! incense. Burn! oils.
Throw out the scents that remind you of her.
Do not say her name.
Knit. Jumpers.
Wrap regret around your throat.
Call it a scarf, not a noose.
Flagellate.
Wear a hat.
In the temple,
Sit.
Sit with quiet.
Sit straight.
Hell is real and you don't always have to die to get there.
Obsess on possibilities.
Fast.
Tithe. Generously.
Confess and seek repentance...
And Pray.
Pray.
Do not, do not say her name.

AM I WORTHY?

Mama I tried
I learnt the lessons you taught me
I tried to live the dream you fed me with hot chocolate, roasted
breadfruit and saltfish –
To do my best in school
Serve God with all my heart
Achieve all I can
And when the time is right, get a good man
And he will kiss my sleeping love and awaken me to the
wonders of the world like Sleeping Beauty
He will come with the glass slipper and I'd be his Cinderella
and it will be a perfect fit
2.4 grandkids later you would have love bouncing on your
knee
And laughing children playing in your living room
You taught me well Mama
Though I saw your hell
I learnt your love
I got me a good man
And I made his life hell Mama
Because, charming as he was, a prince was not my destiny
And I know it hurts you
It kills me inside that I cause you pain
But you gave me life Mama
And above all your dreams for me
You wished me happiness
You wished me love
And my happiness is packaged like us Mama
A strong black woman
With loving brown eyes that look at me with utter devotion
A touch so soft I feel it with my heart, not on my skin
An embrace that presses me to softness
She takes me places I never dreamt existed
Whispers in a voice that makes the world disappear

Love so pure and blessed
Awakens passion in me like a raging inferno
Flying without wings to heaven, and back
My love has curves like we are gifted with Mama
And wields the power of Venus
It's in her arms that I blossom Mama
She makes my tree ache to bear fruit...
It's a choice you made for me when you loved me so well
Mama
The universe has answered your prayers
I'm loved
We walk in the light, Mama
We both serve God
She does not replace you
She does not replace God
I wear defiance as an armour, but a persistent apology as a
mental condition.
A hard-boiled egg with a firm but fragile shell,
a rubbery resistant albumen, a yolk that looks firm, but
crumbles to powder at a touch.
I apologise for the finished product being always unfinished.
Mama, I apologise...
And I forgive myself for all the things I didn't become
I still love you
I still crave your approval
I am still your little girl
I still yearn to please you Mama
But it is not all up to me
She loves me, and I love her...
God loves me and smiles at us.
Mama
Do you love me still?

WHITTLE

I did not come here under a lorry
with bin liners over my head so the
carbon dioxide readers cannot sense

my breath. I did not sail here on a rubber
dinghy and watch my brothers and sisters
become food for sea creatures. I did not

cross a continent over land needing
to buy a new passport and acquire a
new name at each border crossing. I am

from Jamaica. Called the pearl of the
Caribbean Sea. It is beautiful, idyllic.
My land is not torn apart by war. Just

chained by terminal culture norms.
I was on last rites. I bought a ticket, flew
British Airways. Was served vodka and lemon

en flight. Here I am. Tell me your story,
you said. Here is the altar, worship. I
brought me, and you made of me a sacrifice.

Systematically stripped me, peeled back
my flesh and pulverized my bones. Whittled
me down to who I fuck, to how I fuck,

to when I learned what fuck was, to how many
times did you fuck her? What exactly did
you do? Torn apart by need; whittled. Whittle:

To cut small bits or pare shavings from.
To reduce or eliminate gradually.
To cut or shape wood with a knife. Not a

word much used to describe a human being,
but in your eyes, am I human? You taught
me inconsequential. I brought the best

of me, and had to learn that what you really
wanted was no part of me. With your callused
carpenter's hands you whittled me down to

what you find consumable. There, you said,
I have made you beautiful. See how good
I am to you? Here I am. Your Pygmalion.

Your Aphrodite's blessing. Your social
experiment. Your triumph. Don't I wear
your guilty well? Always with the dichotomy

of gratitude and grief. Wracked by survivors'
guilt. I sorrow for fragments of me left
in a land across waters, but it's the

pieces you took that remade me warrior.
A constant itch under skin. I sit on
the fence vacillating between thank you

and fuck you; and knowing even so; I am
one of the lucky ones

VOICES

I hear voices
My heroes
they talk to me
My doctor says increase the medication
I say spread the education
I hear the voices of those who went before me
Saying
My silence will not protect me
I hear uninformed voices
So, I WILL write more poems
I WILL address more conferences
I WILL run more workshops
I hear misinformed voices
So, I WILL tell MY story
Because as long as we let others tell of us
The truth recorded in history
will be their version of events
I hear voices
I see visions, apparitions
Hear angry voices
It's 1969 and it's a riot
Stonewall says no more
People die
Change is never easy
Progress is never free
Human life has forever been acceptable collateral
Ghosts speak to me
I hear voices
Muted, quiet voices
Voices that vote on equal marriage
Voices decide if the respect enjoyed by the masses
To freely enter this union of love
Will be extended to me
We think we are not owned

We think our lives are ours...
While we rightly celebrate how far we have come
in the bid for equality and respect
Let us remind ourselves
our journey continues
we are still a long way from home
I hear voices
I hear voices
Voices I hear that whisper
Voices in my head
voices that remind me I am more
More than just a lesbian,
More than just a woman,
I need more than mental health intervention,
I do not seek validation
I do not seek acknowledgement
I seek acceptance
I command respect
I demand equality
I hear voices
I hear your voices
Do you hear mine?
The voice of frustration?
The voices detrimental to my existence are not voices in my head
It's the voice of the preacher man that damns me to hell
It's the voice of the politician who legislates against my survival
It's the voice of the doctor who medicates my protest
It's the voice of political correctness that looks at me and says it doesn't see colour but clutches the purse tighter when a black man stands close
It's the voice of society that would deny my very existence if I should, for one minute, not use my voice
My right to be, is not another's to revoke
there isn't enough tippex in the world to blot out my existence

I'm here I'm gay I'm fabulous
I hear voices
I hear the voices of the hidden and oppressed
Invisible does not mean non-existent
And as long as I am breathing
As long as I am denied dignity
As long as I am denied MY rights
As long as you are denied
The world will be hearing my voice

Valerie Mason-John

Those Were The Daze

DAZED

There is the daze
And then the vacant gaze
The morning after
A night of hedonistic laughter

Whoever would've thought I'd become an elder of the Black Queer Community? I used to joke that as I aged I would one day be part of the first *en masse* population of out Black Lesbians in Britain. Of course there are my contemporaries, now in their sixties, seventies and beyond, but I believe it's the baby boomers of the '50s, and the Generation Xers of the 1960s and 1970s who are to be thanked for making it easier for the new generation of Millennials to enjoy more of a comfortable black queer life today. And yes, more can be done, because they are still torturing and killing us in some of our countries of origin.

Being out and proud and loud wasn't an issue for me. I had no black family to shame or to keep me in the closet. I was transracially placed in orphanages and foster homes, and so I had a freedom to express myself without the confinements of a strict religion, or the conservative attitudes that many of our communities have inherited from the colonizer.

The colonizers gave us the bible and took our lands. They gave us clothes and enslaved our bodies. They demoralized us and told the whole world we were inferior. They gave us binary attitudes – men/women, heterosexual/homosexual – and made everything else in between illegal, undesirable, and shameful. And today many of us still identify – consciously and unconsciously – with some of these imposed stories.

So I was born, along with many others of my generation, to be one of the torch-holders, and blaze my voice, and put words out there in the world. I first worked as an international corre- spondent and feature writer for the *Voice* newspaper in the '80s. I covered Aboriginal land rights and deaths in custody in Australia, and reported on the tour of Nicaraguan women speaking about the war there. And I even have the polite letter I received from Maggie Thatcher's office after she reneged on a promise to do an interview with me while she was Prime Minister. I was giving talks on panels with John Pilger and Stuart Hood. I was published in the *Guardian*, head-hunted by other newspapers, and so you would think my career was made.

But then I came out in the *Voice* newspaper, wrote an article – under a pseudonym, but my cover was blown, and doors silently closed. I didn't care: I was young, arrogant, and did what I wanted. Lesbian and gay doors opened. I was invited to write the first book on black lesbians in Britain. It was an act of fear. Everyone had an opinion, including me; however I think I got it right in the Black Community.

I invited Anne Khambatta to write with me, because she worked for the Black Lesbian and Gay Centre, and it was important to co-write with a British Asian lesbian because 'black' extended beyond African descent on our lesbian and gay scene. Black included those descended (through one or both parents) from Africa, Asia (i.e. the Middle East to China, including the Pacific nations) and Latin America, as well as lesbians and gay men descended from the original inhabitants of Australasia, North America, and the islands of the Atlantic and Indian Ocean.

We upset the white community by writing that 'all white people are racist'. Would I write that now? No: I would write something more gentle, something people would be more willing to hear, as I do believe that while all white people must have some racism, it's called unconscious bias. Just as I have some racism towards other races of people which I'm not always conscious of.

When I published the second book I edited, *Talking Black: African and Asian Lesbians Speak Out*, the mudslinging began. My publisher rang me up and said something like, 'I warn you the review in *Time Out* is not good.' The review was full of racism, referring to what had been written in the first book in a highly negative way. From that day on I never read a review. However Lesbian Avengers zapped the *Time Out* offices, and it was said that *Time Out* received the most complaints ever about a review.

My lesbian career began. What did I have to lose? I went on to write the box-office sell-out cult play *Sin Dykes*, which explored the current scene of the '90s where black lesbians and white lesbians overlapped. A play for three black women and three white women, it explored the issues of cross cultural sexual relationships, and what happens when you add to the mix a light touch of sadomasochistic sexual activity. With a few rewrites to include the trans and non binary community, this play is still very relevant today.

Even so, I was, as Emma Parker writes, the 'Odd Girl Out' – the title of an interview about me in *Textual Practices* (2011). I was always different, not black enough, too white-minded. However if you talked to many black women in the '80s and '90s, they would tell you their first touchstone for the black lesbian scene in London was one of my notorious parties on Nursery Road, Brixton. They were notorious because they had a diversity of race. South London Women's Centre was one of the few public venues that had a similar space. There were the Black Only lesbian parties that I loved, and there were the clubs and parties which didn't say White Only, but when you had spent much of your twenties picketing outside clubs because they weren't letting you in, what else would you tell yourselves?

I lived on Nursery Road, and often the road sign was graffitied as 'Lesbian Road'. While many of its residents were white lesbians, there were at least four famous black lesbian and gay households on that street. The late Arthur Peters, a fashion designer; Lorna Lee Leslie, the artist; Dorothea Smartt, the Bajan poet, and the African-Americans Pamela Maragh, choreographer of Soul II Soul, and Richelle Dinnigan, choreographer and dancer; and a few famous alternative straight black women lived on this road too.

I'm sure I've missed a name or two, as I was also part of that party culture which took drugs, and I know I lost a few brain cells storing precious memories on my journey.

You could say I began to grow up in my 30s. I became a

Professional Black Lesbian, I was the artistic director of Pride Arts Festival, and then of Mardi Gras Arts Festival. I promoted the National Lesbian Beauty Contest, that was televised on Channel Four and brought Samantha Fox out, and screened the first ever labia piercing. Sadly this great feat brought me into public conflict with club promoter and celebrity Amy Lamé, and it was the talk of most lesbian and gay papers for several months. I went on to co-produce the National Drag King Festival with Jean T and Linda Riley. I ran the largest club night in Europe, Queenie's at the Fridge, for its last year. Before then it had been Eve's Revenge, and Venus Rising, where I rose to fame as one of the go-go dancers.

Jennifer Dean produced what was perhaps my best offering to the mainstream, *Brown Girl In The Ring*, in which I had one hour to prove to my audience that I was related to the Queen of England. Mixing fact with fiction, I convinced my audience enough that still to this day I'm asked, am I related to the Queen? This show went on to tour North America.

I retired from the scene in my late thirties. Noticed when I was first out on the scene it was Lesbian and Gay, and by the time I retired it was either Queer, or Lesbian, Gay, Bisexual and Transgendered. I'm still Black, and I'm still Queer, but these labels are no longer at the centre of my life. Now I'm concerned about the lives of black men, which are being shortened either by the police, or through black-on-black homicides. I'm concerned about addiction destroying our communities, and all communities. I now work as a Buddhist teacher, and as one of the leading African Descent Voices on Addiction and Mindfulness.

Never before has there been such an urgency for Black and Asian communities to rally together. Some of us are Muslim, and many of us have Muslim names, and many of us will be mistaken for Muslim. And with the rise of Islamophobia both communities are under threat. And when we are under threat, our own communities become more conservative and less tolerant of other cultures, and especially of queer culture.

In the 21st century we need to come together and fight for our basic human rights. To be Muslim, to be Queer, to be Trans, Two-Spirited, Non Binary, and Out and Proud.

Tamara McFarlane: eight poems

That Girl

I saw her and she saw me
At first I wondered what she did see,
For a lesbian I was never allowed to be
So in all my life there's been two of me.
I shake all over when at me she smile
And I knew I should've run a million mile,
My country greatgrand said gay is wrong
The pastor said it's an abomination.
I told myself to look away fast
Don't think about this very sweet lass,
But how my goodness she look so fine
And her in my arms would be more divine,
How can they say slavery is done
When bound in chains was how I was born?
They said God made us all in His own image
Then why I a lesbian isn't one of the privilege?
Change the bible create your society
I shouldn't be tortured for your hypocrisy,
God took a part of himself and me he created
So as a lesbian woman I should be liberated.
In every dictionary going back through history
The word gay has always meant happy,
Lesbians, Gays, Bisexual, Straight, Transgender
We all come from one and are one together,
So the next time that pretty eye girl look my way
I will walk boldly over to her and say,
I am free
no longer living in captivity
Was told two, but there's only been one of me,
Out and proud lesbian would you love to dance
We'll take it slow, thanks for the second glance.

Back To Me

A couple more hours
Then it will be midnight
A new year will begin
And new perspectives in sight

As I wait for the closing of the year
My mind journey back to what is now ending
Things and people to be left behind
Broken heart and dreams that need mending

A tear escape down my cheek
As I think of something I have to do
To find someone that have disappeared
The me in my heart that was true

And as the end gets closer
I search for the missing key
To unlock the door of courage and strength
That has been lost inside of me

Fear of Hating

Face lit up
Smiles anew
Thoughts are there
Something to do

Crazed emotions
Filling up space
Bitterness appears
Winning the race

Feelings evaporate
Through sizzling heat
Shreds of hope
Accept defeat

And now proposed
New twist of fate
The greatest fear yet:
Having to hate

Heart Stealer

You knocked
I opened
In you came
Love words spoken

You moved so fast
And you took control
Of my heart and mind
My body and my soul

You wasted no time
Going for my heart
Making it yours
Before taking it apart

Now under your spell
There is nothing I can do
My heart, shattered in pieces
Is now enslaved to you

Loving You

Loving you in sunshine
When my body is cold
The heat from your love
Makes me warm all over

Loving you is honey
When my mouth was numb
I felt the softness of your lips
And discovered sweetness within

Loving you is pain
When I can't be with you
My body cease to function
And it hurts all over

Loving you is caring
When you are hurting
Don't shut me out
I am here to comfort you

Loving you is peaceful
When we are alone
At times not speaking or touching
Simply being together

Loving you is frightening
When I can't seem to stop falling
Harder, stronger and deeper
In Love with you

Loving you is love
To know you is to love
To love you is perfection
And perfection... is heaven

The Body

Curves are form
A masterpiece is in the making
As the body ascend
Into the voluptuousness
Of a woman
Enticing the unsuspecting eyes
That take in every contour
And every rhythm
The body has
Or makes, when it moves
A body full of grace
Informed by the beauty
Of the owner within
A beauty that's unspoken
No words to describe
The free flow of its movement
Gliding like the stars
Moving across the skies
The body that seduces
Without words
Caressing deep within
Without touching
Full of power
Alluring from afar
Taking whatever it needs
To exude
What the body knows
Beautiful, tantalizing, pure
Skin smooth as alabaster
And softer than sheer silk
The body unattainable
A goddess of a body

What I Felt

I felt your eyes
I saw your face
I knew I was wasted
I knew I was daze

I felt your lips
Crushing mine
Tenderly you suckle
Gently you bite

I felt your tongue
So soft so sweet
Tantalizing and teasing me
Until our bodies meet

I felt the movement
Of your finger tips
Setting my body on fire
As before, your lips

I felt our clothes
I knew they were gone
And then we were moving
Together as one

I felt what you gave me
And what from me you take
And in the moment we come
I wonder if I made a mistake

You & Me + Me & You

I close my eyes and I still see you
My blood races to the surface of my skin
Just the picture of you in my head
Is enough to get the wings of my heart to flutter
   Non-stop at each end
   As it beats rapidly
   Fiercely I come undone
But you and only you can make me feel invincible
I want to sing and dance though I am good at neither
On the verge of the heights of the peak of total madness
Your daringly explosive rampant passion rocks my inner core
I am tipping over into sheer bliss
Where you have me at right now
Nestle between your breasts
I watched you move in my dreams last night
And I held you as you came back down to earth with me
So why now that I am fully awake
My mouth savours still the taste of you
My tongue traces the outside of my lips
It tingles with the reminiscence of your beautiful self
And here I thought you and me
Were just a passing forever fairytale.

Clementine Ewokolo Burnley

Forty Flavours

Greythwaite is one of the better schools. Lydia hates the trumpet but it's a big part of how she stays here, on a combination of scholarship and bursary. The parents at the school gates every morning are a mixture of power couples – they drop off in Range Rovers, steering their way around the lollipop patrols, stressed to the eyebrows – and ecological liberals who do something in the arts, and who weave their way around the Range Rovers on pushbikes. The whole collection is liberally sprinkled with single mums like me, and a few rare examples of the stay-at-home parent.

What I notice after plumping myself down on the plywood and metal chair, is the light. Much as I love the bars of Harare, the illumination filtered through veils of cigarette smoke is minimal: you have to wait till you get home to see who you have. Greythwaite school gym is high-windowed and cavernous, the white painted walls and pine floors collecting the brilliance pouring from the LED panels above us, imprisoning the orchestra between reflective surfaces. I have never been the sort of mother who sneaked into school assembly. But it's the last one. This class is graduating in the summer and I do not want Lydia to say I was never there.

It's the movement of her arm that catches my attention. Not the perfect half globe beneath the see-through mesh shirt, the thin arm, holding a phone camera pointed at – I assume – her son – who, by the way, cannot play the saxophone. It's clear she adores him, and that makes me fall in love a little, with them both. She's tall, lighter skinned than me. I want to say, 'Is my gaze okay?' At this stage I'm pretty sure it's objectifying.

'Is that your son?' I ask. When she nods I point to Lydia. It's a pleasure to meet you, Violet Mandéré, she tells me. The double lift of her tongue at the end of my last name takes me home. Women who can pronounce my name usually come from places invaded by the French Empire.

'Enchanté,' I say, trying out A Level French on Celie, whose parents are from Martinique. 'My parents wanted me to learn English,' she says. We chitchat about our children. She looks amused when, deciding I've heard worse, I say, 'Maxime sounds très professionel.'

'I don't think he's found his instrument yet,' she says. 'What brings you two to the Greythwaite orchestra?'

I laugh and ask, 'How much time have you got?' And when she looks at her watch it turns out she doesn't actually have any time at all for me to tell her about the location of Mbare or about Matapi Flats where I grew up.

On the bus home Lydia and I are quiet together. My daughter was eight years old when I left Zimbabwe. She will be sixteen when we return. I don't know Celie well enough to tell her Lydia and I are running from a combination of unrelated things. I was a teenage mother living with my parents and brothers in the married couples' apartments. The accommodations for singles were separate. After I had Lydia it was clear. Being unmarried in Matapi Flats was a problem.

Lydia could read when she got to preschool at four, which surprised her teachers greatly. My mother had been reading to her at home. I knew the books by heart because the hardback Puffins had belonged to me. In Lydia's reading books Dick and Jane played on a carpet of grass. The children threw a ball and the dog Spot ran. Dick and Jane's dad went to work. Their mother wore an apron. Everyone repeated words. 'Run, Spot, run.' That was pretty much the life I thought my parents wanted for me. It's not so clear-cut now in my mind. My brothers spoiled Lydia rotten. She rode shotgun on all their escapades. But I was tired of making excuses for why I didn't want a man, even one who loved me. The gap between my parents and me had grown while I weighed up which truths they could hear. I was in the last year of nursing school when I decided feeling on guard all the time wasn't good for me.

Celie waits a week to call. The voice at the end of the telephone is surprisingly warm to my excited ear. It's my day off tomorrow. She wants to know if I've ever been to Highgate. I say no.

When we meet she is wearing a shade of pink lipstick that,

it occurs to me, would look better smeared against the dark skin of my face. 'Do you know Highgate already?' Celie asks. I say, 'It's the first time I've heard of it.' It hadn't occurred to me anyone would go to a cemetery for fun. 'Ça va?' she asks. She wants to know if I'm okay to go in, so I fix my face and tell her Highgate looks nothing like Mbare West, near where I grew up. Women don't go to Mbare alone, or even in pairs, unless they are walking behind a coffin, or in one. Usually I would feel closed in under the wet branches but my mind is full of Celie. Wandering along the twisting paths I tell her about my job here and how I've always wanted to travel. I'm curious about Martinique, but Celie says, 'I don't know it really.' She adds, 'I've always lived in London.' Celie works for a logistics company in Streatham. 'It's very boring.'

The sun goes behind a cloud, which on cue spits out rain. She's brought two umbrellas. The wet muffles the sound of footsteps on gravel, so when the old couple appear through the arch of a massive tombstone I flinch. I say aloud, 'It has atmosphere.' I tell her I'm learning the British art of irony. What I really meant was that it might be haunted. Her laugh is quick. 'Oh, if we are out before dark we should be safe.'

Celie remembers where we left off outside the school. She was really listening. I tell her Lydia and I moved to East London. Not moved, so much as jumped in a colonial lifeboat after a disagreement with Uncle Bob Mugabe. For us there was no quick immigration scheme conjured up at a high political level in Whitehall as there was for the Rhodesians. We were the wrong part of Britain's imperial past. It's just as well I had a nursing degree.

I ask about her family. Celie's grandad died in his sleep at forty-nine. Her dad is forty-four. Since finding out about this family history, she's made a series of bargains with his heart: not killing spiders; not adding powdered ginger and chilli, which she loves, into her spice mix for fried plantains; and saving arguments for the very early morning. 'You must think we're not all there.' I don't.

We're sitting on a bench absorbed in conversation when the blunt nose of an SLR invades my peripheral vision. One end of the camera is pointing at Celie and there is a tourist at the other. I am aware of the cold across my bum when I stand up.

The bench is of course damp despite the newspaper Celie brought to sit on. I put my palm across the lens and say, 'Who's this?' There is already pain at the thought of anyone else looking at the feet falling out of stack-heeled espadrilles, the angle so steep and the footbed so wide her thin toes are caressing the grass. It turns out the woman is charmed by the sight of two black women in the park, heads together, and asks how long we have been best friends.

'Parlez vous Français?' I say with a heavy accent. She doesn't seem to speak French, so I continue. 'We no speek English.' The woman gives up and wanders off looking offended. Celie's eyes are scandalised.

'You're my first Zimbabwean friend.' she says. I feel mild disappointment. My experience is that friends have time when they need something and none when they don't. 'Havarari friend,' I say. I'm not sure about wearing a whole country around my neck. I tell her Harare is a restless city, haunted by English ghosts and wide-awake women. She says, 'I didn't learn anything about Africa at school.' Lydia isn't learning anything either and some of the things she tells me are not good. A bunch of children chasing her friend, flipping up her skirt, shouting 'lezzy'. I'm the kind of person who thinks problems are best left behind.

'Can they?' she asks.

'Can they what?' I say, not understanding.

She repeats, 'Be left behind?' I didn't realise I'd said that out loud. It seems weird, so I don't answer.

I tell her I like East London because Lydia has Aliz and Sue. When we met, Aliz wore their hair in coloured rubber bands, listened to K-pop all the time, and never slept, coding payment systems for businesses in three time zones, saving for the lease on a small shop. Lydia has learned to drink cardamom-spiced milk before bedtime from Aliz, and taught me which pronouns Aliz prefers (they, their).

Sue is a pug. You can hear her panting up the stairs from three floors down. I'm not too good with dogs. I'd liked Aliz ever since they'd replied to my fretting, 'She won't bite, will she?' Aliz had said, 'Who? Lydia... naaah! And if she does, the vet's just down the road.' We'd both cracked up.

When Aliz signed their lease Lydia painted a watercolour

called *Forty Flavours, by Aliz*. There are brown and black figures looking through the stained glass windows of an ice cream shop.

Celie's phone is vibrating like mad from the bottom of her bag. It's Maxime, her son. When she hangs up I assume she needs to leave and can't think how to tell her I'd like to see her again. Instead Celie announces Maxime is staying at his grandmother's in Brixton. She takes my hand. 'Want some ice cream?' I ask.

We walk by Forty Flavours without stopping. Lydia goes there every day after school now. At my place I make Celie tea and change my damp leggings for tracky bottoms. When I come out of my bedroom she's taken her shoes off. The skin of her calves is smooth, disappearing too soon under an unflattering animal print. On my tongue her toes would taste dusty. Of forest paths, inner lips of black liquorice and happiness. I could walk away from truth again. Instead I say, 'Did you know butterflies taste with their feet?'

Germaine Joseph: 3 poems

Sleep

As you sleep
our heart meet
Asking the questions that lovers do
Like would she marry me
Does she feel the same
And when we make love
Does she like it that way

As you sleep our souls meet
We ask each other questions
About our separate rebellions
Are you here for the long run
Are we good enough
Could our lives be stuffed
Can we be that tough

As you slept our eyes met
Asking ever still
Searching
Searching
Searching for something still
Searching for peace
Not wanting anything ill to happen
To this
Duality
Your Fragility

When you awoke
We combined
Synced our pussies with time
Unison
Union
Slippery
As you kissed me

Tasting of the finest wine
As you slept all I wanted was to protect you
Ingest you
Tell you that you're perfect
Even when you're crying
Hug you even when your whining
I'll love you
Even when you're tired

As you slept
I cried
I'm a baby
But I take pride
Coz you're my only
I'm selfish
But you captivate me
Even as you sleep

I adore you...

Snippet

Your presence shimmered on my soul
We talked all night
About our lives and hopes
Fears and ultimate wants
Dreams...
You smiled
Your smile lingered on my eyes
And danced on my heart as it beat
It was cold
We got under the sheets to cosy down, to feel the heat
Continued speaking on past lives
Putting the world to rights
Passing ideas, debating our fears
Well into the night
Until the first thrustings of light
Intruded the space
Making way again
For your most stunning face

Jammin

Recently I been jammin with the sun singing with the moon

Even with the stars I been making tunes

This earth's protecting even when it's all going wrong

The clouds are giving me proverbs about what's going on

The trees are always dancing, always encouraging to be free!

The grass gave me a cuddle as we cuddled under the cacophony of this beauty

Surrounding me

Recently I been blowing with the wind, it's always making jokes with me, we been taking trips together to far and distant lands

The earth took my hand, smiling we came together chatted and broke bread together

Matter enveloped me took me to see galaxies

And surrounded by this awesomeness

I remember how sweet life can be

Black holes may be scary but beyond we can find undiscovered galaxies

The universe speaks and I know for sure this higher energy it's got me.

It's got you.

It's holding us

Life is precious Be.

Monica Beadle in conversation with Rikki Beadle-Blair

This is a conversation between out black gay film- and theatre-maker Rikki Beadle-Blair, at time of recording 55 years old, and his Jamaican-born mother, out lesbian Monica Beadle. Rikki is eldest of five siblings, (in order) Gary, Carleen, Nathan and Nia. Monica raised her family in Bermondsey, a white working-class district of South London.

Rikki: I wanted to ask you, who was the first gay person you were ever aware of?

Monica: The first gay person I was ever aware of? It gets – there were rumours of people at that time – there were my friends and neighbours who were around, so we were just learning about that kind of thing – but I remember the one that came to me was Dusty Springfield. I loved Dusty Springfield. If you remember, I had a big picture of her... *(sings)* 'you don't have to say you love me'...

Rikki: *(laughs)* So did you have a crush on her?

Monica: Not consciously, at first, but eventually it was conscious... There was another woman I had a crush on at school, but I didn't realise it was a crush until a bit later, when she had left the school. She was a teacher – the classic talk that you would say about P.E. teachers, and I realised I really had a crush on her. I was really into sport – netball; and I was a sprinter, you know, a real Jamaican way of up-bringing with the sprinting – I was very athletic.

Rikki: And do you remember anything about this teacher?

Monica: Yeah, her name was – maybe I shouldn't say her name –

Rikki: I think you can...

Monica: *(laughs)* Her name was Miss D. I always hated it if I had to miss a session for whatever reason, or she wasn't in. Most of the time for the sports sessions she was the teacher, and it was like my teenage years, that sort of time, so, secondary school. And I remember afterwards, looking back, a couple of years after she left – she'd been there a few years – she was getting married, having a baby – something like that – and I was so sad, so heartbroken. And there were lots of teachers that I really liked, but – it was afterwards, when I started to learn about gay people, that I realised that's what I had felt: a proper teacher's crush that people talk about, on the sports teacher.

Rikki: You came to Britain when you were eleven, and this was a crush when you were – thirteen?

Monica: That sort of age – thirteen, fourteen. It was secondary school, so less than sixteen. Between twelve and sixteen.

Rikki: And a bit later than your crush on Dusty Springfield?

Monica: Yes, because – around then: it was a continuation – I loved her voice, and I loved her look. And there was something touching about her voice that was very black. She had that kind of soul voice...

Rikki: And when did you know you had a crush on Dusty?

Monica: There was a point after leaving school of thinking, yes, I love this woman. I was aware I felt really, really drawn to her; really embraced her.

Rikki: And did you – there were rumours going around about her right then.

Monica: She was mid- to late-sixties, but after I left school the rumour was that she was going out with Madeleine –

Rikki: Madeleine?

Monica: Yeah, Madeleine Bell. She was a black American singer.

Rikki: She was amazing; she was in the band Blue Mink –

Monica: She went to live in France –

Rikki: She had that huge hit, 'Melting Pot', which I love to this day –

Monica: Yes, she – she's been living in France maybe thirty years now –

Rikki: And they were a couple at the time?

Monica: That was the rumour. They were close – there were pictures – and I saw them at the Flamingo.

Rikki: What was the Flamingo?

Monica: A club in Soho. It was called a jazz club but it was really a music club. And also Madeleine and her went to the Roaring Twenties, which was a black nightclub in Carnaby Street.

Rikki: And you used to go to these clubs?

Monica: Yes.

Rikki: Wow, so you were Miss Swinging Sixties...

Monica: *(laughs)* Yes. I used to meet people, friends of mine, and go down, cos a lot of South-East London, the guys we knew from Brixton and Peckham, used to go down to the Roaring Twenties to listen to the reggae music and soul music.

Rikki: So you'd all put on your make up and try to look older to get into all the clubs?

Monica: I don't remember – perhaps we looked eighteen; I think by that time we probably were old enough to go in the Roaring Twenties when it got really swinging.

Rikki: So what was the first gay club you ever went to?

Monica: It was a club-restaurant in High Street Kensington, and my friend Darryl, who's passed now, and a Jewish girl – we used to be really good friends, you remember?

Rikki: Yes, very well.

Monica: She had that white car – and he had a friend, one of her friends, who was this gay guy, and there was a place where mostly gay men went, and you could eat, and downstairs they had a club going. So we used to go there, because there were more places for the guys to go than the girls.

Rikki: The friend was Leon, wasn't it?

Monica: Exactly. The hairdresser.

Rikki: He was right in the middle of everything, wasn't he? He was full of life.

Monica: And she had the white Capri, do you remember?

Rikki: She drove it onto the estate and Bermondsey Street –

Monica: Yes, Whites Grounds...

Rikki: Do you know what happened to Leon? Obviously you haven't seen him for a long time –

Monica: I did hear that he had passed, quite a few years back now. I think from my friend Heather, who was involved with... they were close.

Rikki: So what was the first lesbian club you went to?

Monica: The Gateway.*

Rikki: The legendary Gateway?

Monica: The legendary Gateway, in Kings Road.

Rikki: Can you remember what it was like?

Monica: It was packed. It wasn't huge, but it was packed, lots of people dancing, and people – some people – changing, especially if they wanted to wear what's known as their butch clothing. Change their dresses into what they wanted to wear.

Rikki: So they would come in looking girly and then be themselves when –

Monica: Yes, and there was sometimes a queue, because there were only one or two loos – and put on, if they liked wearing trousers and jackets, because that's what they would say they were – the butch and femme thing –

Rikki: That's amazing.

Monica: – because that was one of the easier ways of contacting people, because it was very obvious. Unlike now, where people are more likely to dress how they want to dress: you can be butch, but you don't have to wear more masculine clothes. But back then that was one way of people identifying who was butch and who was femme.

Rikki: Was it very much a butch and femme scene in there?

Monica: Yes. Because that was where they could really be themselves in private.

Rikki: What was the music like?

Monica: It was music of that era. There was some soul music, some pop music; it wasn't hard-core anything, you know?

Rikki: Did you dance there? Did people dance?

Monica: Oh yes. Oh yes. We danced. But that was the era where a lot of people danced very stiffly – you can see that in *The Killing of Sister George*. I wasn't around then, when they were filming that; that was a bit before –

Rikki: How did you feel to be in there? Were you scared the first time you went, or nervous?

Monica: More a bit nervous the first time. But then I started going regularly, and I got on really well with the women who ran it, though there wasn't many of us black people – black women.

Rikki: What was your first Gay Pride march like?

Monica: It was great. The first one I didn't go on the march, I watched it from the Southbank. We hung out there because it began somewhere in the middle of town and ended at the Southbank. They came over Waterloo Bridge.

Rikki: And this was would have been the eighties?

Monica: Yes, and it was nice because it was on our side of the river; it wasn't hard to get to. Then it moved about. It went to Clapham Common at one point, and then Hyde Park. But how I knew about it was, I used to know this woman in South London, quite elderly; and there were five of them – two women and three men – and they met – you know the place – on the grass at Islington, near the tube station –

Rikki: Between Upper Street and Essex Road, yeah? *(door-buzzer)* – Hold the line, one second... *(Rikki goes to sign for a parcel, comes back)* Do you mean Highbury Corner?

Monica: Yeah. They got together there and got talking, and little by little a committee –

Rikki: So at your first Pride march were you surprised how many people were there?

Monica: I was surprised it was happening. I don't remember how I first heard of it but I did, and I went down and really felt very at home, and it's really – it's comforting when you see others, other people and know that, Yes.

Rikki: Is that why it's important to you to go? Because you go every year, and you go to other Prides too, and to Black Pride.

Monica: Yes, and it's just like how Black Pride started, you know? It's two people saying – and it really helps to open it up and help those who are struggling to meet people: it can be a way – even if they're really closeted, they can be out there on the streets and have a look and see what's going on.

Rikki: It's so important. So –

Monica: ...and leaflets are handed out, so they know yes, I can go to this club or this pub; they have a meeting upstairs. Cos a lot of it used to go on in the Notting Hill area – running from Marble Arch down to there, they had little pubs where people used to have meeting places upstairs where people could – you just wanted to meet other people.

Rikki: Where you could talk and just connect.

Monica: ...and find strength. And look at what it's grown to.

Rikki: Did you think you would ever see gay marriage?

Monica: We talked about it, but it seemed like it would be another era, and we wouldn't be around, maybe, to see it. And we talked about equality, and I've always felt – and I talk about that – it's the same battle that we had about race and gender. And we battle on; and that's the thing about people putting in their time and strength, and sometimes laying their lives on the line for equality. We're all different, but we're all equal.

Rikki: I know you were too young to think about politics and sexuality then, but you visit Jamaica every now and then. How do you feel it is for gay people there? I know there's an image...

Monica: They fought – that's why you have J-FLAG** – and it's a smaller place, but people do live there, and they are gay. People get attacked, but it still doesn't stop it. And the hope is one day it'll really be established. It's certainly come a long way, but there's still a long way to go.

Rikki: I remember you telling me about people who managed to integrate themselves into their communities. I remember you telling me about how people would talk about Uncle So-&-So or Auntie So-&-So, but there'd be an understanding amongst families...

Monica: Well, people felt they knew or suspected, but they weren't chucking them out or beating them up because of it. But still they couldn't be too flamboyantly out –

Rikki: They had to be discreet.

Monica: Yes. But it was known, and in certain communities – some of the people who identified as gay, or who were identified as gay, they were helpful to the community: they needed them too, for whatever work it is that they did, you know? Especially when you're living in those little communities, especially not in the cities – but even in the cities, in the poorer areas, you need someone's help: they're a doctor, or a teacher; they can help you fill in forms or help you do this or that. So you soon learn it'd be foolish... It's like that old phrase, 'cut off your nose to spite your face'.

Rikki: When did you realise you were gay? Was there a moment of revelation?

Monica: The revelation was the fact of wanting to go to somewhere like the Gateway and remembering it, and it was more about reading books and hearing things, and you'd see things, and it started clicking for you, and that's when I decided, 'Oh, I remember that place where the all those women go, and they dress like men and...'

Rikki: And it started to fall into place.

Monica: And I went to the Gateway. Because we lived across the street in a hostel.

Rikki: Who's 'we'?

Monica: You and I. Because in those days different boroughs used to help each other. You could be living in Lambeth, or Southwark, and there could be a hostel in Islington, or West London, and so you'd be placed there. Because lots of homeless hostels were really spread. That's how a lot of my friends met people: they'd say, where do you live, and they'd be placed in South London but really they'd be from North London...

Rikki: I remember you telling me about watching a TV programme with a friend of yours and there was suddenly a big moment for you – sitting in your bedsit and –

Monica: Yes, that was in Nunhead. I don't remember the programme, it may even have been *The Killing of Sister George* – something like that; and watching it and watching it, and following it and following it, and it was really a dawning moment. And we turned and we looked at each other, and we kissed. And that was really acknowledging it.

Rikki: And when did you realise I was gay? I'm one of five children, and the oldest, and I'm the one who's gay. Was there a moment?

Monica: Well, there was a moment. But the first time it was said out loud was when your teacher asked me, how would I feel? Because I think he must have overheard someone calling you something in the playground – a name. And he asked me: how would I feel? And I said –

Rikki: That was when I was in state school, right? So I must've been under eleven.

Monica: That's right, the one up in Dulwich.

Rikki: Dog Kennel Hill?

Monica: Yes. I remember that teacher. He really liked you. He thought you were so bright and intelligent, and he asked to see me, and he asked me, and I said, 'That's my son, I love him for whoever he is.' And I was really shocked, because you'd never told me you were bullied about it.

Rikki: So did he call you in?

Monica: Yes. He was very supportive – who knows, he might've been gay himself – very embracing – and he had the assumption that I would probably go crazy. So he wanted to suss out, if you came home and told me you were being bullied, to see what my reaction would be. Because he might've experienced parents that were very homophobic.

Rikki: Was that the one who said he thought I might be prime minister one day?

Monica: Yes.

Rikki: What was that story?

Monica: He was just chatting about your intelligence, acknowledging you were a very bright student – your skill with reading and book-knowledge – 'He could be the first black prime minister,' he said. And the vacancy's still open!

Rikki: Realising I was gay, when I was an adolescent and when I came out, did you worry it might not be safe for me?

Monica: No, never – not that I recall.

Rikki: Was that because we had so many problems with the racists that –

Monica: I think that overtook it, because that was so much in the news: the race thing, rather than the homosexual thing.

Rikki: Because I remember, just after I moved out, you had to move, didn't you, because of the amount of racism – they tried to burn down the flat. Can you tell me about that?

Monica: That was in Bermondsey. Yeah, they came and put fireworks – it was Bonfire Night – they put fireworks through the letterbox. It was the same guy who'd scratched my Mercedes – and I thought, what if there was something there that could've caught alight? But indirectly it worked in our favour, because we got to move into a nice, brand-new house.

Rikki: And there was that thing, do you remember, when they put [younger sister] Carleen in a dustbin?

Monica: Yes. That was that same: it was one part of that gang. The bins at the back had no lids, so they lifted her up, and –

Rikki: Shocking.

Monica: – and it was the same lot. [Your brother] Gary'd remember his name.

Rikki: He will. But somehow you weren't worried that I would get problems for being gay. Was it that I had the right vibe?

Monica: Well, I *was* worried, but to me it wasn't that obvious, and there were no incidents going on to worry me. The only time I had anything it was in the home: one of your friends had come round, and I pushed the door open and the two of you had been kissing, and you pulled away. Do you remember that?

Rikki: Wow. That must've been Andrew.

Monica: Yes.

Rikki: And you caught us! *(laughs)* He was trouble, but he was my first love. Did you worry I was gay because you were?

Monica: No. It didn't worry me. I sort of – if anything, you think: not surprised. These things are a gene, you can't take it on. It's in you; it's part of people. That's why so many people are struggling when they come out: because of all the oppression and prejudice they fight it and keep it down, until one day they let it all out. And that's from fear. And then they say, I've known since I was six, or ten, but just suppressed it. You can shut things out of your mind, but there's a time when it just comes out. It's easier for people if they're around it. Nowadays it's still difficult for people, but it's easier because it's a lot more open, even with all the prejudice that's still going on.

Rikki: There's a lot more of a sense of 'what's the big deal?' going on, so...

Monica: ...and you feel a bit more safety in numbers.

Rikki: How do you feel seeing young lesbians now, out on the streets, holding hands?

Monica: I feel optimistic about the future for all of us, and there *are* those ones, but just like with other prejudices, with black people, with race – the same thing with gender, how us women have had to [deal with it] – that does make us stronger, and it helps the others that are coming behind – the more of us there are, whatever the issues, whether it's race, sexuality, or gender...

Rikki: So do you feel you're part of the ladder that's there for younger people to climb?

Monica: Yes, and there's more of them that are really stronger than in my time, who are able to feel more – and that's a good thing: it shows that yes, we have made progress.

Rikki: You used to work in a homeless advisory unit –

Monica: A young people's project –

Rikki: – for homeless people around the King's Cross area. Did you encounter many lesbians there?

Monica: There were some. For sure. And there are some that I see now, and I remember how they was when they first came...

Rikki: How does it feel being a bit of a lesbian icon now?

Monica: *(laughs)* Oh, I embrace it.

Rikki: Everywhere I go, gay women always say to me, 'I know your mother!'

Monica: I know, I know. *(laughs)* I've got people saying to me, 'If we go out, or walk down the street, or go in shops, or we go out all night somewhere and nobody knows you I will be dead shocked.'

Rikki: Do you feel like London is your village in a way – that so many people know you?

Monica: They really do. And I have to put my hand up, I do know lots of people and it's not just through the gays: a lot of people just know me.

Rikki: Is that because you talk to people?

Monica: People give me so much stuff... I think it is because I talk to people, and I smile at people, or I'll help them out or something. But lots of people have said there's an aura around me that draws people – like if they're going to pick on someone to ask them something, the chances are they're going to ask me. And people say they love my smile – they feel like it's genuine.

Rikki: It's something all of your children do: we all smile a lot. Where does your smile come from? You don't complain about what you've gone through, but you've had to work hard to build a good life for yourself and your family.

Monica: The smile comes from my heart, and the way I actually was brought up. It's about being warm to others, and thinking about others, and being genuine. One phrase going on when I was a child was, 'it could be me'; or, 'it could be you'. Some people think they're above things happening to them... What we would like for ourselves, we should be thinking of giving that to others. And you want people to be nice to you, and smile at you, and help you if they can. And you can't just want it, you have to give it. 'Do unto others...' I used to hear that at Sunday school time, when I was a kid.

Rikki: If you had your life to live over again, would you still be a lesbian?

Monica: Oh yes. You make it sound like I chose to be, but I wouldn't want to be born a different way. Because I know it's a gene thing: it's not like I decided, like 'I decided to be a footballer'; it's not like that. But no, I wouldn't [change that]: I want to be me. And the world is very diverse in all ways, as are us humans. And who we are is who we are, and we shouldn't have to be – there are some people setting an agenda, saying we should all be that – No: what we are is what we are. And I do believe we're born like that, but sometimes it's suppressed and there's something that brings it out in people – yes, you can have some people decide to exploit it because they see if they're that in a certain situation, because you always get that in life. But for most people in life, that's who we are.

Rikki: That's who you are.

Monica: ...and I do believe that's how we're born. A lot of people who study animals see those traits – of differences. It's the diversity of life.

Rikki: Well, I'm glad you're who you are. Thank you so much; that was a beautiful interview.

Monica: Thank you.

*The Gateways club was a noted lesbian nightclub located at 239 Kings Road on the corner of Bramerton Street, Chelsea, London. It appeared as a backdrop (including extended scenes filmed inside featuring regular club-goers) in the 1968 film The Killing of Sister George, *starring Beryl Reid, Susannah York and Coral Browne, one of the earliest mainstream films to feature lesbianism.*

**J-FLAG is the Jamaica Forum for Lesbians, All-Sexuals and Gays, which campaigns for the repeal of British colonial-era anti-sodomy laws in Jamaica, LGBT equality generally, and runs gay pride events on the island.

Olivette Cole-Wilson

After Alice

Life isn't the same anymore; it just isn't the same. Sometimes I feel really angry; bitter... Why me? Why Alice? Why now? They don't prepare you for this at school or college. It's a bit like having children; you're just expected to get on with it, and if you're fortunate enough a few kind souls will give you a hand along the way, especially in the early days; mother, father, sister, close friends – but society doesn't prepare you for motherhood or fatherhood, and it certainly doesn't prepare you for death.

I was really bitter at first, bitter and twisted. I hate to admit it now, but I would even look at people on the odd occasion when I went out to the shops and think, why are you here, why aren't you dead? I know it must sound terrible, but I was distraught and everything was really distorted.

It's been four years now; sometimes it doesn't feel like it's getting any better, but I suppose it is. I've started to smile again, and I've even laughed a few times recently.

The other day I had a good belly laugh. I found something Alice had made for me. Fortunately I was at home on my own – if anyone had seen me they would have thought there was something seriously wrong with me. You know when you laugh at something hysterically, to the point when you are hurting and tears are streaming down your face; the kind of laughter that can't be forced, real, rare? That's how it was, and the thing is I know only Alice and no one else would have found it even remotely funny.

I know she would want me to move on now, be out there having some fun. I can't. Not yet.

We used to talk about moving to our 'lavender home'. We assumed it would be quite a way off, and that things would have changed for the better by then. We even discussed names for the home; 'Lavender Ladies' or 'Delightful Dykes', or maybe both; and next door in the same grounds there would be the Gregarious Gays or the Diva Queens. Menus would include tofu and halloumi cheese, though we did wonder if they would still be fashionable then; and of course there would be rice and peas, curry goat, jollof rice and chicken.

We imagined joint tea dances, singing round the piano, oral history sessions and storytelling, our own *Come Dine With Me*, and even make up classes – though probably more for the men, (although I've noticed how some lesbians, as they get older, are using more make up; maybe from a tiny hope that this will defy the aging process. Maybe I will too).

Anyway, all of that is lost now. Alice and I won't be spending our last days as we imagined.

She's not here now to spend those precious moments with me; well, not physically, anyway, but she is with me all the time, mind you: in my thoughts, in my dreams, in my head, in my heart.

Doreene Blackstock

The Missing I in You

There is no **I** in You
I observed on this particular morning
As **I** stood, hovering at the front door.
Then the epiphany!
Which **I'd** never noticed before
The absence of the letter I in the word blame
Funny that.
The **I**, I felt in bewildered made me cry.

There's an **I** in pain
Of that **I** am certain
It's identical to the **I** that weighs heavy in the word strain
As my eyes search for reasons across your face
Again and again and again and again
Once my kissable face
Once my familiar
Once upon a time – my heartspace – my home – my lover.

There is no **I** in the word pretend
Or the word who? Who is she?
Or the word when? When did you both meet?
Or the word how? After 18 years was it so **final**! So complete?
Denial, **she** was no friend
Tore off the band aid
Removed my rose tinted specs
Pulled up the blinds
Let the light in and shone the sun directly in my sights...
Bitch! There are five stages of grief.
What's the rush with this Tsunami?
I wish there was a visible I at the end of the word why?

There are three **I**'s in responsibility
There is one in the word choice
There's an **I** in smile

Ooooh
And there's a hidden **I** in the verb sigh
Funny that...
How heartbreak can be Sooooo tiring.
So needy
So unattractively hopeless
I couldn't stomach myself – the pleading
Begging! Begging! **Begging!** Me? Begging?

There isn't an **I** in surrender
But I surrendered
I crumpled to my knees and I surrendered
I let go!
It was Ugly. I was Broken.

As I tried to hold my world together that appeared to be
haemorrhaging out of the slits in my face. Cascading down my
chin
Tears hitting the floor like the **I** in ping!
Only not melodic...
The sound was flat, harsh, desperate – wounded – wounding.
The echoes of which fell on deaf ears where she sat at the
kitchen table
Our first purchase together from **I**-k-e-a
Arrogant – Poised – Unyielding – Stone
Reading the Sunday broadsheet
Fingers Fat, Nails cut short, self-taught manicured neat –
Butch!

There is no **I** in this **We** anymore
Hiss
In this You and Me anymore
Hiss
The missing **I**... **ME** in **you** is for real!
Hiss... Hiss... **Hisssssssssssssss**

Roxene Anderson

My Type

You want to know my type?
Well here's a clue of who she is
More than a one dimensional list of adjectives
She lives...
My strength is melted by your lips
As they curl at the ends and my favourite place at your cheeks
dip
I'm hit, by the lack of temptation by any other chick
I know what I've got and wouldn't risk it for shit
Cuz you're it
Beyond a visual representation
Or a physical sensation
Our minds fall into an allied elevation
The air is thin but pure up here,
Your motives are clear
And I feel safely vulnerable
Not seeking your other half, you're already a whole
I feel blessed beyond control,
With my clichéd soul... mate
You drop everything, including me
When you're needed by your family
Driven by success
Yet perfectly flawed
Your elegant aura keeps me in awe
This is beyond sex, the physical is more complex
The expression of our obsession
Engulfing the gentle and passionate aggression
Only exhaling when your pleasure is in my possession

And then you can rest
I'll sleep with my heart in my arms
The only alarm will be your waking surprise
Whether it's the feel of your eyes or your breath on my thighs
Every morning I want to rewind and feel that moment again

'Nea Semba'

Supermalt, Self Love and Sexuality

We are more alike, my friends, than we are unalike.
– Maya Angelou, Human Friend

I would like to preface this by saying that I am not an expert on intersectional feminism, nor on the many aspects of black queerness. Merely, I am a participant in black womanhood and its accompanying nuances, so many of which are subtly placed in the 'other' category.

I share my experiences in the hope that it helps someone else along on their journey to finding themselves. Initially I felt anxiety and apprehension at baring myself so discernibly and I'm finding it sobering.

I write this cautiously and discreetly as I still hold an internalised fear of rejection and violence. The reality is that non-white queer people have to be withheld out of anxiety that they will be exiled for being honest.

At the time of writing, I have not yet 'come out'. The premise of coming out to me has always been wrapped around an internalised discomfort at having to explain that my being, everything that IS me, is still stagnant despite my wavering sexuality.

That and why is it anyone else's business?

Often, I liken my 'coming out' (again, in quotes) to a boiled egg: You're not sure if it's too soft, or if you're panicking because it might end up being inedible.

Was I queer before or did my queerness come into existence once you read these words? Which came first?

Consider this, this wall of text, this clumsily strung-together cluster of eccentric metaphors, analogies and half-stories, my Soft Boiled Egg, here for your ingestion.

Don't Touch My Hair

Solange, in the song 'Don't Touch My Hair', describes her hair as her feelings, her soul, her rhythm, vision and crown. There is something deeply rooted and unifying about black womanhood and hair. The two exist in a symbiotic relationship. Doing your hair, whether it's intricate and/or time consuming or simple, reciprocates energy back to black womanhood; lending themselves to each other to for the sake of maintenance, and trailing into a desire to represent an identity. Put simply, it can reflect your position in a social subculture... or demonstrate an intention to conform to – or renounce – assimilation.

Why am I bringing up hair? In order to discuss lifting the curtain on the intersection of blackness and queerness, we need to discuss them as separate entities, to avoid whitewashing of either issue. Queerness is wholly seen as 'a white thing'. Blackness is seen as tough, hard and unyielding.

I've made my share of questionable hair choices; the most memorable was a relaxed hairstyle, cut to shoulder length and dyed jet-black, that earned me a homophobic range of Sapphic-inspired nicknames. These were most often spouted by infantile teenage boys who reeked of overbearing Lynx bodyspray and juvenile sweat.

Secondary school was a cesspool of cruel, determined brutality and almost everyone was lost in it, and almost everyone was complacent in making sure it was carried out.

In the echo chamber of the playground such mockery was only a fraction of the kind of savagery that placing value on what was deemed 'normal' gave rise to. Fear of 'the other' and all that. Despite this, there were some silver livings and positive experiences I took away with me.

I ran in different circles of friends, and in North London diversity wasn't a token South Asian student forcing an indentured smile on the front of a school brochure promising multicultural unity, but an effortless reality.

In my class of 30 there were people from the farthest reaches of the world, myself included. My friendship group consisted of mostly girls; twins from Afghanistan, two (unrelated) Turkish Cypriots, a Mauritian girl and me.

Even though I spent most of my secondary school life with

non-black girls, I never felt like my blackness was called into question or my assertion of it discouraged. I have had a lot of qualms and negative experiences with this friendship group – to the point where all we are right now are just +1s to meagre follower counts on Instagram – but when it concerned my blackness, I was supported, and in the very few moments where I put it myself on show – for example, when I first discovered what my hair looked like when I shook it out, I was applauded.

Of course, my first real violent experience with my natural hair, usually put away in tidy, neat braids that my mother, aunts or cousins had tirelessly worked on, also occurred in secondary school.

Often, the contentious battleground for the right to choose how black femmes present themselves is fought in a 'professional' environment, and for most of us, we learn what is appropriate for 'professional' environments from school.

My first perm came after months and months of my eleven-year-old self begging. Little did I know this first trip to a salon bordering on Edmonton and Tottenham would be the first step on a tumultuous journey of self-hate, self-discovery and, ultimately, self-acceptance. At least, for me.

The next day, as I flipped and shook my twenty-something inches out, split ends and all, I was the centre of attention. I felt like Naomi Campbell, strutting as confidently as I could down the primary school corridor. I remember being surrounded by my year's 'it' black girls, telling me how beautiful and sleek my straightened hair was. Those many hours in the salon, held hostage under a hair-drier, were worth it. It was that kind of positive reinforcement that led to years and years of leaning on the box of relaxer whenever my roots started retreating back to their coarse, kinky texture.

This, coupled with hearing 'this is your grandmother's fault' from my cousin as she ripped through my thick hair with a wide-tooth comb, added to the load of self hate that led to me denying my blackness.

On my mother's side, almost all my cousins and aunts have sleek, 'manageable' hair. My mother had loose, shoulder-length, bouncy, kinky curls, but as she matured she stopped wearing it natural. So I grew up seeing my mother, whose facial structure is mimicked in a browner shell, with different hair to mine.

My mother retains a heavy value on her blackness, strengthened by her status as an 'other' when she had to leave Africa to assimilate in Europe. She was born in Africa and, even though she's been on British soil for longer than she was there, she still asserts her status as a headstrong, fierce African, and still serves her country's government in London.

She would tell me stories about how people mocked her for speaking how she spoke, with her heavy African accent weighing her words, but she told me she had a lot of pride in her identity, so she never let it bother her.

Although she is very light skin, often white-passing, (depending on where she is – for example, African people can tell she's not, but Europeans seem to have difficulty in noticing the distinction), she has never wavered in her loud, expressive way of exhibiting her pride in being African.

In my mother's family, my aunts and uncles range from having deep, dark skin to being almost white passing. However, their hair type usually ranges from 1C to 3C, maybe 4A. Often my cousins were mistaken for South East Asian simply because of how sleek and long their hair was.

When people talk about homophobia, when it comes from the black Diaspora they usually focus on religion, not toxic masculinity and the leftovers of colonialism. Homophobia in this context is a lot more nuanced because of the history of a more tolerant and relaxed culture around sexuality and gender pre-colonialism.

In the *Guardian*, Ugandan LGBT activist and journalist Val Kalende describes homophobia as a 'colonial legacy' (Kalende, 2014) and discusses this in a more extensive way than I have room to do here, so feel free to peruse my citations and seek out the article. The prominence of homophobia in all its glory did little to stifle my approach to banishing homophobic phrases and ideologies from my household. I do believe that in being able to do so without fear of retaliation or exile, I am greatly privileged.

*

Food For Thought

I grew up having heated debates with my family, in particular my father. When he first came to the UK in the '80s he could barely speak English, and when the time came in the early '90s for him to recite his wedding vows, he did so mumbling awkwardly in English. When he began to assimilate into the culture, learning from working-class white British males, he picked up on the gay bashing lingo.

I grew up idolising my father and craving his acceptance. My favourite thing about him was (and still is) the long-winded anecdotes and pearls of wisdom he would share with us on long car rides to our grandmother's or to local farms. However, often he would point out gay couples or effeminate men and describe them as 'poofters', make snide comments and limp-wristed gestures to express his disgust.

Over the years, particularly at secondary school, I started unravelling my own internalised feelings towards gender and sexuality, and started thinking independently. I was always outspoken, and many a time I got into arguments with boys who tried to deem me weak or unable to kick a ball around because of my gender. I like to think that I was born to be a feminist and it was always going to be my path.

When I was around 14-15 I started hanging out with a small group of friends who were mostly queer or, if not out at the time, made it known that they were, at the very least, LGBT allies. My parents were always very kind to my friends, and I would bring them over for dinner or to hang out and play board games.

In 2009, I attended my very first pride. I admit, during my 'revelation' that I was part of this community, I was lowkey fetishising of gay men in my desperateness to be accepted. I did the whole 'wanting a GBF' phase and outgrew it to see why it's so important to have that kind of education implemented, especially for young people.

I attended my very first pride with two black friends who were in queer relationships and identified as lesbians at the time. They both attended the same Catholic all-girls' school, and later on re-identified their own sexuality as bisexual/queer.

My parents were upset about me attending, but they weren't going to lock me away in a tower.

I remember leaving my house, and my mum asking me where I was going at the door. I shout-mumbled something along the lines of 'Pride' and ran to catch my bus before she could tell me not to go. I could hear her call after me, 'Why are YOU going to Pride?'

Over the years she repeatedly tried to 'catch me out', though each attempt was more comical than invasive – and hey, Mum, if you're reading this, I knew that you knew!

I would constantly correct my parents and, over time, they grew out of their ignorance – in particular my father, who now sends me LGBT memes and talks positively about the progression of tolerance of LGBT culture in Europe.

Naturally, he does need me to check him every now and then, but overall he is nowhere near as toxic or as flagrant as before. Baby steps.

> *I write for those women who do not speak, for those who do not have a voice because they were so terrified, because we are taught to respect fear more than ourselves.*
>
> *We've been taught that silence would save us, but it won't.*
>
> – Audre Lorde

Black femmes are always accused of trying to appeal to Eurocentric ideals for wearing Malaysian bundles. Black femmes with shaven heads are told they lost their beauty with their hair. We can't win either way.

In most free-to-play games, you have the 'starter' items. If black womanhood was a free-to-play, the starter hairstyle would be braids. Intrinsically, these styles were ways for us to manage mounds of hair – but as time and fashion evolved, they became entwined with cult trends, particularly in the 2000s.

Now we see a revival of natural hair: it's become a movement – as history tells, our hair has categorically always been politicised. From Creole tignons to combed-out afros, there is always a narrative of jealousy; rebellion; and deviating from what we've been told is the pecking order, as decided by centuries of 'upselling' Eurocentric features as superior.

The birth of the Black Girl Magic movement is inclusive; it validates all black girl identities, not just a heteronormative, one-size-fits-all one. When you have figures like Janelle Monae and her two-tone declaration of embracing her carefree black girl status, and Solange demanding a seat at the table, it's difficult not to feel animated.

In an alternate world where I am 11 in 2017, maybe I would have never begged for that first perm that led to a decade of tumultuous self-doubt and questioning. Maybe, just maybe, I would have felt the unambiguous tranquility I feel about my existence today, much earlier.

But then again, hindsight is always 20/20.

I have an unyielding belief that representation leads to more open doors than magazine cut-outs stuck on diaries and beautifully put-together cosplays on Instagram, and is about determining a deeper value in ourselves. Which is explicitly critical to building the framework for a new generation of resolute, unashamed, profound black girls, who will go on to break boundaries and shatter glass ceilings without feeling an apprehensive impulse to hastily glue the pieces back together, to seal their true selves in for someone else's comfort.

For black women, existing virtuously as ourselves is an act of protest. We defy age-old prejudicial conventions; we embolden each other without applying age-old prejudicial censorship. Be loud, be brazen, and dare to be something distinct and unprecedented until it becomes the norm.

I came to the realisation that I was non binary before I knew there was a word for it. I always thought it was my natural 'off-ness' and let it be. It wasn't until I started joining intersectional feminist groups on Facebook that I heard of it.

Initially I joined because I needed perspective on my dissertation, which was centered on feminism and lad culture and how – and if – the two can co-exist. I ended up staying because of the friendships I developed – even though I ended up not interviewing anyone from any of the groups I'd joined. It led me to a brand-new term (to me) to describe what I had been feeling for a while; non binary.

Now, popular culture will tell you that non-binary feminists are just 'attention seeking weirdoes' who want to find something new to be enraged about. For me, the issue with non-binary-ness is that people expect you to have a certain look. I can't really approach the androgynous look because I'm a top heavy, plus size femme, so for me, my existence as a non-binary person, like my sexuality, is discreet. That, and I feel like how I look is non binary enough because *I'm* non binary. And that's that.

I remember when my best friend was discussing gender and sexuality with her Black British and Nigerian colleague at university, and he asked specifically what 'non binary' was and meant. At first he assumed the stereotype; that we're all neon-haired weirdoes, pierced to the nines and wear all black. One out of three isn't bad. I do suffer in the summer though.

She showed him my Instagram. For context, I have large brown eyes, a youthful face accented by high cheekbones, dark shoulder-length 3c hair and, as immodest as it sounds, I'm considered conventionally attractive. He instantly retracted his comment, and I like to think he learned a lesson about assuming tropes set by dudebros as gospel.

When I was younger I had trouble with the way I dressed. I used to peruse men's clothing, and drowned my frame in fabric to conceal my curves and to feel more masculine. I didn't shed my cotton exterior until I was twenty and became more comfortable in my body.

This idea that me presenting as femme makes me less queer and less non binary was almost self-imposed, but was also encouraged by a culture that, I'm sorry to say, *is* performative in some sense. It's difficult to explain, but it's kind of like when you go to an Iron Maiden concert wearing a Justin Bieber shirt. You bought your ticket, and you're there to enjoy the music, but because you're not 'conventional' to that subculture, you're instantly harangued and cast aside as phony.

I also remember when I tried everything in my power to eliminate my core characteristics in order to be seen as more feminine, more graceful.

Retrospectively, the ultimate, most powerful resource I had that helped me gain a grip on my identity were the friendships I developed and grew out of, particularly in school. For me secondary school was most definitely the melting pot that scoured off all the little edges and introduced me to a wider worldview.

Primary school was rough. From early days at primary school I was viewed as the 'other', not because of my racial ambiguity, but because I was always slightly 'off'. Luckily, I had my two best friends who were equally as weird, sharing my love of creepy vampire games and other geeky behaviour. As I matured, so did the way I viewed friendships and how I navigated socially through each individual group.

It was an unnerving adjustment to go from having an intimate trio to a whole posse. I became friends with all sorts of groups: 'alternative' kids who wore their fringes over their eyes and listened to metal and emo music; the 'urban' group, composed of Black African and West Indian kids who would argue about socio-politics, ranging from the correct way to say 'plantain' to heated discussions on slut-shaming.

Then there was my class. We were always the 'safe' class. If anyone was going through bullying or having trouble adjusting, they'd get sent to us and they'd either mellow out or become part of our family. That was my favourite thing about secondary school; the mutual understanding. Not to say we didn't occasionally have our issues, but as a whole my class was harmonious. I was blessed enough to go to a school where there was a mosaic of nationalities and cultural identities. My closest friends were from Mauritius, Afghanistan, Cyprus, Greece, Guyana, Bulgaria, etc. Among many other things I got to learn about Islam in a more authentic and correct way than a textbook could ever teach me.

Which leads me to this. I was apprehensive to be open about my sexuality because, although I knew all these things about my friends, I was scared that they would reject me out of a learned prejudice.

When I first came out I was fifteen, and I had known for two years that I was also attracted to women. I came out to my most intimate group of friends first. I answered their questions, and we had our exchange of giggles, but the experience was liberating and I came out of it (no pun intended) feeling positive.

Everyone has this idea of university – that you're going to join all these great societies and make lots and lots of friends. Unfortunately it didn't work out that way for me. I always seemed to attract drama or trouble from the 'normal' crowd, and so once again I sought comfort with the 'others'.

I found one of my best friends on Tumblr, under the tag for my university, and he was the catalyst towards me being 'woker', finding my truth in my blackness and affirming my sexuality.

I also came across a few queer/non binary/trans 'others'. One of my few regrets about university is that we didn't hang out – individually or as a group – until after we had graduated.

Anyway, during my third year I ran for the position of LGBT officer and I ran uncontested, so naturally I won. I was the representative for my campus, and I was expected to work cross-campus with the other campus rep for events, etc. During my campaign my mother called me, after seeing my poster on Facebook advertising my intent to represent the LGBT society, and asked me why I was running – a nudge towards me coming out. I squirmed and laughed my way out of the phone call, which was uncomfortable, but like all her other attempts, comical and light-hearted.

When I attended the very first meeting after being elected, I knew it wasn't going to work. I found myself having to explain biphobia to a white gay man (the other representative) and then had to argue about racism – he was pedantic, and I was already exhausted from nerves and lack of sleep. Later I realised that university positions were a farce, especially since my agenda wasn't taken seriously, despite the very real need to move beyond hosting excuses to binge drink under the guise of expressing 'gay pride'.

I wasn't given any resources or any real power to actually help make a change. The other representative was only inter-ested in hedonistic male-centric tacky parties with unoriginal themes – whereas in my first week I found myself being asked for advice on transitioning by an autistic student.

I'm proud to say I did everything I could to support this student, using my free time to visit them at their halls and give them whatever meagre advice I had to offer, but I felt helpless without backup. I ended up leaving my post two months later and returning home to London.

I wasn't about to be someone's token.

My legacy is this: my existence is resistance. I refuse to comply to norms, I refuse to be silenced, I refuse to apply my self-worth to other people's expectations. I live, in my discretion, in my unobtrusive truth as a queer, black, non-binary femme, all in sync, maybe not as balanced as I would like, but it's comfortable.

I encourage you to stay honest; you, the 'other'.

References and other reading:

Kalende, V. (2014). 'Africa: homophobia is a legacy of colonialism' – the *Guardian*
https://www.theguardian.com/world/2014/apr/30/africa-homophobia-legacy-colonialism

Blain, C. (2017). 'The political rebellion of being black and non-binary' – *Daily Xtra*
https://www.dailyxtra.com/the-political-rebellion-of-being-black-and-non-binary-73646

Ziyad, H. (2016). '10 Personal Rights That I, As a Black, Non-Binary, Queer Person, Refuse to Compromise On' – *Everyday Feminism*
http://everydayfeminism.com/2016/03/black-non-binary-queer-rights/

Qasim, W. (2016). 'Being a black, British, queer, non-binary Muslim isn't a contradiction' – the *Guardian*
https://www.theguardian.com/commentisfree/2016/jun/20/black-british-queer-non-binary-muslim-isnt-contradiction

The problem

I thought you were butch, she said. Tried hard to mask the disappointment my ultra-not-butch presentation of self offered. She had chatted me up online and I had agreed to meet her.
Really? I countered; why?
You always have such strong opinions and speak up so stridently. Somehow my mind just pictured you butch...

P.J. Samuels

Mojisola Adebayo

Everything You Know About Queerness You Learnt From Blackness: Introducing The Afriquia Theatre of Black Dykes, Crips, Kids and All Their Kin[1]

Blackness, queerness and performance are inseparable for me, and my teacher was the greatest, Muhammad Ali. When the heavyweight champ, athlete and activist danced on his toes and declared, 'I'm as pretty as a girl', he was playing with people's perceptions of what a black man could be. Ali troubled gender stereotypes and racist beliefs about black masculinity being monolithic, inarticulate, savage even. He would not slug. He danced – backwards – did magic tricks and recited poetry, until they took his licence away for refusing to go to Vietnam and shoot his fellow brown-skinned man. When he changed his name and his religion, from Christian Cassius Clay to Muslim Muhammad Ali, he undid the idea of what an American was supposed to be (today Trump's government would probably not let one of their greatest heroes into that country). Muhammad Ali was a master of self- and re-invention, a quintessentially queer quality. Ali was heterosexual, but he showed me that blackness and queerness do not need to be seen as sparring partners, but can be seen as dancing partners. And the music Ali loved to dance to most of all was that of a high-camp 'crip' queer black man known as Little Richard. I loved Little Richard so much as a child I named my first teddy bear after him: somehow this South London baby dyke knew he was my kin.

Critical and creative black queerness is about unboxing binaries, blurring boundaries, exposing the mythical norm, messing with form, being in the process, playful, political and, most of all, performative. That's what got me writing plays. *Muhammad Ali and Me* is a semi-auto/biographical piece tracing the parallel lives of Ali and his fantastical friendship with Mojitola, a girl child growing up in foster care in London, surviving abuse and coming out as a lesbian thespian.[2] The queer kid and the Muslim man physically impaired by Parkinsonism become a fictional family in *Muhammad Ali and Me*.

Their bouts are refereed by British Sign Language performer Jacqui Beckford, who creatively interprets the words for D/deaf people. The show was a hit when it premiered at Ovalhouse, London in 2008, and I have been playing with the relationship between black and queer experience, including disability, ever since. I call my work Afriquia Theatre – African Quia/Queer.

I am going to share two extracts from my most recent Afriquia Theatre plays, *I Stand Corrected* and *Asara and the Sea-Monstress*. These plays in very different ways create accessible spaces for black/queer/crip togetherness, understanding, debating and challenging the recent intensification of homophobic colonial laws and violent acts across the African continent and the Diaspora. Both feature female protagonists, are set in Africa, and link homophobia to colonialism. Both challenge the state and criminal in/justice and, most importantly of all, both projects, with workshops, talks and writing around them, seek to nurture in their audiences a sense of black queer *ubuntu*.

Ubuntu is an ancient Southern African, Zulu and Xhosa word for which there is no precise equivalent in English. It means our lives are dependent on, and reflected in, one another – or as Muhammad Ali said to graduating Harvard students when asked to give them a poem: 'Me, We' (the shortest poem in history). When applied to discriminations around race, sexuality and disability, *ubuntu* holds a very powerful message. African scholar Lebamang J. Sebidi cites a lyric by popular South African singer/composer Brenda Fassie, 'Umuntu Ngumuntu Ngabantu' ('a person is a person through other persons') as having helped to 'popularise what forms the very kernel of *ubuntu* as this basic orientation[...] that one's humanity, one's personhood is dependent upon one's relationship with others'[3]. I want to do in theatre what the brilliant Brenda Fassie, a black lesbian artist and activist, did in music, by championing *ubuntu*. I want to make spaces for black queer people to see our experiences reflected, and for non-black and non-LGBTQIA+ people to gain more understanding, empathy and solidarity with us, and celebrate us. Anti-apartheid spiritual leader and campaigner for the rights of LGBTQIA+ people in South Africa Archbishop Desmond Tutu writes: '*Ubuntu* is the recognition of humanity in one another. This is not just a nice thought or sentimental set of words in South Africa. *Ubuntu* is our defining concept: *I* exist because *you* exist.' So too, *ubuntu* is the defining concept of Afriquia Theatre.

Afriquia Theatre is informed by the exciting burgeoning discourse of black/queer theory that has emerged over the early 21st century in such notable anthologies as Delroy Constantine-Simms's *The Greatest Taboo: Homosexuality in Black Communities* (2011), E. Patrick Johnson and Mae G. Henderson's *Black Queer Studies* (2007), Sokari Ekine and Hakima Abbas's *Queer African Reader* (2013), and E. Patrick Johnson's *No Tea, No Shade: Writings on Black Queer Studies* (2016). However, these books largely contain theoretical writings from African and/or American perspectives. There has been very little discussion of black queer theatre and performance from a British queer/performance perspective, which is dominated by white voices that pay surprisingly little attention to black artists. (*Staging Black Feminisms* (2007) by Britain's only other black British lesbian theatre scholar, Dr Lynette Goddard, is an important exception.) As theatre scholar Victor Ukaegbu asserts: 'British queer theatre is white, not black and, though tolerant of black performers, it hardly serves black concerns.'[4] Despite this, and despite the marked ambivalence in black studies towards black queer theatre, he adds that 'black gay performances have been flourishing underground'. In the past few years we have seen a locally active, and internationally resonant, radical black/queer cultural renaissance and political resistance happening on London stages in particular. From fringe theatres voicing the margins, such as Ovalhouse and the Albany, to iconic main houses in the history of British political theatre such as Theatre Royal Stratford East and the Royal Court; from small spoken word events to nationally recognised arts centres of the avant garde, black queer performance is becoming, and coming up strong in Britain.

Afriquia Theatre is inspired by the work of my black British/British-based performance-making ancestors and peers who include Rikki Beadle-Blair, Jackie Kay, Valerie Mason-John, Christopher Rodriguez, Joy Gharoro-Akpojotor, Ade Adeniji, Le Gateau Chocolat, Antonia Kemi Coker and Tonderai Munyevu, Paul Boayke, Kofi Agyemang, Reuben Massiah,

Dorothea Smartt, Dean Atta, Stephanie 'Sonority' Turner, David Ellington, Tarell Alvin-McCraney, Jacqueline Rudet, Deobia Oparei, Steven Luckie, Inua Ellams, Topher Campbell, Zodwa Nyoni, stand-up comedians Stephen K. Amos and Gina Yashere, and leading scholar of black-British theatre, Dr. Lynette Goddard; and this essay seeks to counter the racism of the global gay left that permeates queer theatre and perform-ance studies. Through Afriquia Theatre I also hope to go some way towards addressing what feminist performance theorist Sue-Ellen Case has called the queer erosion of lesbian repre-sentation, by positioning lesbian stories centre stage. I write in part to give more parts to women, black and disabled actors. Representation in all respects is an important function of my work.

Thomas DeFrantz writes in *Black Performance Theory* (2014) that blackness is 'the manifestation of Africanist aesthetics' and that 'This black is action. Action engaged to enlarge capacity, confirm presence, to dare'. African theatre scholars Osita Okagbue and Kene Igweonu call this black action 'performativity', and assert that African theatre and perform-ance 'is not just entertainment but is often geared towards fulfilling particular social or aesthetic functions – hence it is performative at its core'[5]. A recurring feature of black perform-ance is the desire to bring something into being through the act of doing, whether through ritual or activism, towards educa-tion, empowerment and/or social change. As performativity is a key concept of gender/queer theory, it can be used as a frame through which to view blackness and queer experience to-gether.

Paul Gilroy writes that, in everyday black life '[s]urvival in slave regimes or in other extreme conditions intrinsic to colonial order promoted the acquisition of what we might now consider to be performance skills'[6] – citing African-Americans such as Ellen Craft, who escaped from slavery through trans-vestism; and performing white and playing straight in everyday life is a phenomenon practised by both black and queer people. Performance elements such as mimicry and the mask have become defining features of black experience, and demonstrate the damaging effect these affectations can have on the psyche and behaviour patterns of the colonised. Black and queer performance modes have been both instruments of harm and instruments through which liberation has been fashioned – and, indeed, been made fashionable. Camp, at the nexus of performance and fashion in contemporary western black and queer cultures, is possibly the most prolific and high-profile, defiant and flamboyant, mode of cultural expression that we share.

From the fast fingers and hair flicks of rocking and rolling Little Richard to the shaking bananas on the booty of Josephine Baker; from the high flat-top of Grace Jones to the high heels of RuPaul; from the purple reign of shoulder-padded, stiletto-heeled Prince to voguing at drag balls from Harlem to Liverpool, who can say where queer begins and black ends? Or where crip sensibility ends and queer performance begins? Little Richard recalls: 'The kids didn't realise I was crippled. They thought I was trying to twist and walk feminine. But I had to take short strides cos I had a little leg[...] The kids would call me faggot, sissy, freak, punk.' Little Richard performed his body, scorned as 'deformed', as the ultimate dandy. And where would white gay boys have been since the 1970s without the dance floor anthems of black divas, performatively bringing into being the feeling that, as Sister Sledge sang, 'We Are Family...' We – black, queer, crip people – are family, indeed.

Diaspora, as both a material experience and a concept, is constantly evolving a map where blackness and queerness interconnect. DeFrantz and Gonzales write that 'Diaspora is continual; it is the unfolding of experience into a visual, aural, kinesthetic culture of performance' (2014: 11). Diaspora has been intrinsic to black cultural expression, ever since the forced movements of slavery and the chosen movements of migration transported the rhythms of West Africa to the West Indies and on to West London's Notting Hill Carnival. Eve Sedgwick writes that queer too 'is a continuing moment, movement, motive... The word "queer" itself means across'. Like Simone de Beauvoir's conceptualisation of not being born but becoming woman, Paul Gilroy has written that 'Diaspora accentuates becoming rather than being' (1995: 24). Cindy Patton and Benigno Sanchez-Eppler have linked Diaspora and queer becoming, stating: 'Sexuality is not only not essence, not timeless, it is also not fixed in place; sexuality is on the move'

(*Queer Diasporas* (2000: 2). The struggles for black emancipation and LGBTQIA+ equality are movements. We have fought by moving our bodies and acting out our passions, protesting and performing on streets and stages across oceans and seas and we have only just gotten started!

I am a British-born Danish-Nigerian. My performance work has taken me all over the world, from Antarctica to Zimbabwe. The extracts of Afriquia Theatre shared below have travelled to Accra, Beijing, Belfast, Berlin, Birmingham, Cape Town, Huddersfield, Liverpool, London, Singapore and Soweto. They have been performed by black/queer/disabled artists from across the Diaspora: from Cape Horn to the Caribbean, from the Bight of Benin to the island of Britain. They move globally online and now they travel through you. In a time of increasing persecution of LGBTQIA+ people on the African continent and in the Caribbean, coupled with the ongoing battle against HIV/AIDS – a shared African/Diasporic and LGBTQIA+ struggle – it is all the more important to recognise and acknowledge that black and queer are a/kin and to find creative ways of nurturing *ubuntu*. I begin with *I Stand Corrected*, a love story.

I Stand Corrected (extract)

I Stand Corrected (ISC) is a collaboration between dancer/ choreographer Mamela Nyamza and me as playwright, actor and co-director. It was first performed at Artscape Theatre, Cape Town, South Africa, in August 2012, with design by Rajha Shakiry, lighting by Mannie Manim and music supervised by Debo Adebayo of Mix 'n' Sync, and had a London premiere at Ovalhouse Theatre in 2012. *ISC* is a response to the so-called 'corrective' hate rape and violence against lesbians and trans-men in South Africa, and the anti-gay marriage voices in Britain that directed so much emotional violence against LGBTQIA+ people on these islands. The play features Zodwa (Nyamza), a black South African lesbian woman who (we later realise) has come back from the dead, arising from a rubbish bin on what was supposed to be the morning of her wedding, after she has been raped and murdered in a township alleyway by a group of homophobic men who want to 'make her straight'. Zodwa/Nyamza uses dance and movement to explore physically what it means to be a 'corrected' woman. Charlie (me) is her British bride-to-be, worriedly waiting at the altar of a township church hall in front of the wedding guests (the audience). Charlie goes out to find her lost lover, and in this excerpt she is returning to the wedding hall, where she directly addresses the guests/audience. The excerpt can be played as a duologue or as a solo, with Zodwa brought alive by Charlie's imagination.

CHARLIE: I've just come from the police station. Do you want to know what the officer said?

ZODWA (*as policeman*): 'She probably went to find an African man to marry her instead'.

CHARLIE: I said, *what?*

ZODWA (*as policeman*): 'She cannot marry a woman, it's unnatural, this thing, this thing...'

CHARLIE: ...and slurps his tea. I said, 'We are supposed to be flying to London in an AEROPLANE. But I guess that's unnatural too, isn't it? People, flying in the sky like birds.' Zodwa always says...

ZODWA: Charlie, if God had meant us to fly, he would have melted wax on our backs and fixed on feathers!

They both laugh.

CHARLIE: We're going to miss our plane... the policeman says:

ZODWA (*as policeman*): 'It's not our culture, it's not African.'

CHARLIE: I said, well we are getting married today in an *African* church. But now that I think about it church isn't very African either, is it? There's nothing African about Christianity.

The DJ/Stage Manager, apparently offended by what Charlie is saying, tries to interrupt her speech by bringing in Township Funk music. Charlie fights back by rapping/playing with the text on the mic as Zodwa dances in a crumping style.

CHARLIE: Well Jesus was Jewish, except all the paintings make him look Dutch! The irony is, my parents, my 'white adopted parents' that is, helped bring Christianity to this country. Met in Africa as missionaries in the 1960s. Spent their honeymoon soaking up the sun on 'whites only' beaches in Cape Town. Had a splendid time and Daddy even made money in the mineral mines. Made an absolute killing in phosphorus.

ZODWA (*as policeman*): 'What?'

CHARLIE: Phosphorus, you know, the stuff on matches? I presume that's how a humble vicar and his clinically-depressed wife could afford to give a private education to an abandoned brown baby in Stratford-upon-Avon. Except all I was interested in was playing cricket!

DJ gives up the battle and brings the music down slightly.

CHARLIE (*more gently, looking at Zodwa*): And *that's* how I got the chance to come to Cape Town myself, where I met my girlfriend – my *fiancée*: Zodwa Ndlovu. AndILovyu. It's how I remember the spelling. I'm taking her name. Charlotte – Charlie Ndlovu. My birth mother actually named me Donna. I fantasise that my dad was in the West Indies cricket team. Donna Ndlovu. Got a ring to it don't you think? He doesn't even pick up his pen but gulps back his tea, licks his lips and proceeds to stare at my non-existent cleavage. Well, I lean forward to give the police officer a closer view: Yes my white daddy came back from South Africa whispering all sorts of stories about what the savages got up to in their huts.

DJ, offended again, jacks the music back up.

CHARLIE: Oh sorry, have I offended your African sensibility? You don't think white people invented sex like they did aeroplanes do you? Sorry to disappoint you but apparently Africa is the cradle of civilisation so all these same sex shenanigans must have started somewhere. I think you'll find that being a lesbian is as South African as Rooibosch tea!

Music cuts. Charlie moves away from the mic and into the space, now having a conversation with Zodwa in her mind.

CHARLIE: People like my parents imported *homophobia* – not homosexuality. And the Europeans brought all kinds of other clever inventions with them – concentration camps, genocide...

ZODWA: ...apartheid.

CHARLIE: Are those things African too?

ZODWA (*as policeman*): 'It's in the Bible! It is forbidden!'

CHARLIE: – Well so is eating PRAWNS!

Charlie and Zodwa start to gently act out getting into bed, using Zodwa's wedding dress as a bedcover.

CHARLIE: Working on a Saturday, sitting next to a woman who's on her period and a baby boy still having a foreskin dangling after he's 8 days old – not to mention biblical justifications for the slave trade – but let's pick and choose the rules shall we? Stuff the tricky bits in Leviticus about menstruation, shellfish, slavery, Sabbath rest and excess penis flesh – let's persecute the sodomites instead. Well, I don't know about you but I've never been that into sodomy myself. No, I know I have tried lubrication – the officer's eyes start to widen. But I hear anal sex is an excellent *heterosexual* contraception. Particularly popular with the Catholic population, you should try it sometime – but always use a condom won't you? (*Gently, to Zodwa in bed*) Unnatural, I'll tell you what's really unnatural. Forcing your cock into a woman's cunt. That is unnatural, that is un-African. So are you going to look for Zodwa Ndlovu or not?

Charlie and Zodwa fall asleep for a moment then jump up, back to reality, Charlie at the mic addressing the guests again.

CHARLIE: Now the policeman doesn't seem too happy about my tone of voice. True I could have been a bit more diplomatic but it's been a very difficult day, and as the beads of sweat are crystallising around his crucifix he looks deep into my eyes... deep into my eyes... And I have never felt so white...

Excerpt cuts to: Charlie on her knees whispering into the mic, hands in prayer position as Zodwa moves on top of the bin, her back to the audience, in a stylised sequence drawing on the moves of a cricket umpire. Fauré's Requiem *plays softly.*

CHARLIE: The policeman says... 'I think you still have time to catch your plane back to England.' Ah yes, our pretty little island. We actually wanted to get married in my father's parish. Mum might have even got up from bed to bake us a cake. The only problem is Daddy is one of those angry Anglicans who stands in his pulpit on a Sunday morning to preach that gay marriage will destroy the Church of England. Ironic coming from an institution that was started by Henry VIII – a man who murdered two of his six wives and broke from the Pope because he wanted a divorce. Still, he did invent cricket and that's evidently all I'm good for. Poor Dad, and he thought he was singeing his white guilt by adopting a little half-breed nigger like me. What a disappointment I turned out to be. What a waste of all those minerals. So we would have got married in England, but we can't. *(A beat. Music snaps out. Charlie grabs the mic now like a stand up comedian, while Zodwa pulls at the wedding balloons)* Personally I blame the royal family. You see, if they allowed gay marriage it would mean a queen could marry a queen *(they laugh).* Then where would we be? No no no, a faggot in the royal family would end up as dead as a...

ZODWA: Dodi.

CHARLIE: That would be even worse than Princess Diana marrying an Arab. A Muslim?! They'd have to put the brakes on that one. So that's why we decided to get married here, in South Africa, the rainbow nation, symbol of forgiveness and reconciliation, where equal rights are enshrined in your glorious constitution. Except it's not that simple is it? So tell me, nice Mr Policeman, where are we supposed to go? Perhaps I should thank you: if this were Nigeria, Uganda or just about anywhere else in Africa *I'd* be the one under arrest. Are you going to look for her? *(Silence)*. Where is my wife? Go home... I think everybody should just... go home.

Charlie exits. Zodwa draws a face on a balloon – the face of her killer. She now realises what has happened to her.

ZODWA: I stand corrected. Is this what you wanted?

Asara and the Sea-Monstress (extract)

Asara and the Sea-Monstress is a play for children from four years old up to adults. It had staged readings at Birmingham REP in 2012 and at the Albany Theatre in August 2014. I wanted to find a way of talking about homosexuality and homophobia, through an inclusive, accessible black aesthetic, with small children, their families and friends. I decided to work through metaphor. *Asara* is about a left-handed girl growing up in the mythical West African right-handed Kingdom of Dexphoria. *Asara* addresses homophobia, discrimination and difference through the metaphor of left-handedness, merging African and European myths and folk tales. *Asara* is also the first all-black British cast to integrate performers who are disabled and deaf and to creatively integrate British Sign Language. In this way, the play merges 'crip', queer and black theory and practice, challenging what Robert McRuer (in *Crip Theory: Cultural Signs of Queerness and Disability*, 2006:8) has termed 'compulsory ablebodiedness'. McRuer urges that we need a postidentity politics of sorts, but one that allows us to work together; that acknowledges the complex and contradictory histories of our various movements, drawing on and learning from those histories rather than transcending them. *Asara* is about working together and if, like some of the actors in *Asara,* you are black and gay and disabled, McRuer's approach is all the more crucial.

In this excerpt, Asara has drawn the winning portrait of King Dexter in his new 'robes'. Dexter has been tricked by witches into wearing an outfit that can only be seen by the very brave and the very wise (he is wearing nothing at all, his nudity disguised by playful stage blocking). Asara goes to sign her portrait with her left hand, and is arrested for doing so. The only one who might be able to save her is the powerful Sea-Monstress, a girl named Toshun who did not want to marry Prince Dexter and so gave him her literal hand in marriage instead. After chopping her own hand off, she bathed her bloody stump in the river, fell into the water and transformed into the Sea-Monstress. Dexter was so angry with Toshun that he made being left-handed a crime. But the Sea-Monstress is still secretly worshipped by the left-handed witches who believe she will one day save the kingdom. This is the scene where Asara is put on trial.

COURTIER: How do you plead?

ASARA: Not guilty!

COURTIER: Barrister for the Prosecution.

BARRISTER (*Bows to KING DEXTER, turns to ASARA*): State your name.

ASARA: You know it already.

BARRISTER: For the record.

ASARA: Asara Tennant.

BARRISTER: A little unusual isn't it?... Asara... Apparently the origins of the word are *(looking at his evidence)* 'troublesome, sinister – left-handed'.

ASARA: Well I didn't name myself!

BARRISTER *(Looking up at MAMA and PAPA in the gallery)*: Indeed.

ASARA: Anyway, it just goes to show I've been this way since I was born.

BARRISTER: So you admit to being left-handed?

ASARA: I'm not a criminal! I demand my rights!

BARRISTER: Left-handedness is not a human right but a human *vice*. It is not normal.

ASARA: It's not normal to be right-handed, it's just COMMON. I bet there are lots of left-handed people out there just like me...

ASARA looks to the audience, engages them through improv – 'is anyone else left-handed like me?' If anyone responds, BARRISTER improvises: 'you'll be on trial next' etc.

COURTIER will bring the court to order.

BARRISTER: Using your left hand is perverted!

ASARA: But WHY?

BARRISTER looks uncomfortable.

BARRISTER: It is only to be used for... dirty jobs.

ASARA: What jobs?

BARRISTER: Big jobs.

ASARA: Well let's ban them too shall we? *(ASARA marching*

and chanting)
Ban bums, ban bums, prosecute all who poo!
If you do do-do then we'll do for you!

COURTIER: ORDER!

GUARD restrains ASARA.

BARRISTER: Left-handedness is of the other side. Over there they even drive on the left side of the road and read and write from left to right – it's absurd!

ASARA: Maybe I should go and live with them then!

MAMA: Don't send her away!

ASARA: Why not, Mama? Life would be a lot easier. Do they clap with both hands over there because I like doing that as well YAY!

ASARA claps with both hands – also illegal.

BARRISTER: You see, everything about this creature is un-natural!

ASARA: If it's so unnatural how come nature doesn't have a problem with it?

BARRISTER: Explain?

ASARA: Bring in Majit the cat and I'll show you!

COURTIER: Call Majit the cat!

MAJIT is brought in by the WITCHES and given milk to drink. He drinks then dips his left paw in the milk and licks it.

ASARA: See!

YAGI *(Asara's friend)*: Way to go Majit!

COURTIER: Silence!

BARRISTER: This despicable practice is not acceptable in the human race!

ASARA: Well then I'd rather be a cat! Meeeeow!

BARRISTER: A sign of witchcraft! She works against God.

ASARA: I was made this way!

BARRISTER: You are left-handed because you love to sin! You are just an insolent exhibitionist!

ASARA: Well at least I don't prance around in public showing off my privates!

KING DEXTER: I've heard enough! CHOP IT OFF! CHOP HER HAND OFF!

MAMA & PAPA: NO!!!

GUARD takes ASARA down from the stand and drags her to the executioner's block. She struggles. YAGI runs up to the WITCHES.

YAGI: You've got to do something!

WITCHES: Sea-Goddess! Sea Goddess! Witness injustice! Witness injustice!

The SEA-MONSTRESS rides in on a huge wave.

WITCHES: TSUNAMI! RUN!!! *(Everyone scatters)*

GUARD: What about the girl?

KING DEXTER: Lock her up in the tower!

LORD LAND: Come on!

To sum up

So black dykes, crips, kids and all your comrades and all your diasporic kin – the future of Afriquia theatre is yours. This is your beginners' call. You've got the likes of Muhammad Ali in your prompt corner. In you I see the curtain fall on all mythical compulsory normativities. Play on, with more pleasure and more power than ever before. May your theatres be places of *ubuntu. Amandla awethu!* – the future is yours!

These Afriquia plays and critical writing form part of my practice-as-research doctoral project at Queen Mary University of London (QMUL). I gratefully acknowledge the support of QMUL and my supervisor Dr Catherine Silverstone and my advisor Dr Caoimhe McAvinchey. Extracts from these unpublished plays may not be performed in public without permission from the author. If you wish to perform them, or if you require full manuscripts, contact me directly on mojisolaadebayo@hotmail.com.

Notes:

1. This essay is largely drawn from my chapter of the same name in Alyson Campbell and Stephen Farrier (editors) *Queer Instruments: International Perspectives Where Performance Leads Queer* (Basingstoke: Palgrave Macmillan), 2015, pages 131-150, reproduced by kind permission of Palgrave Macmillan. I gratefully acknowledge my editors Campbell and Farrier, and Palgrave Macmillan, for the re-working and re-publication of substantial parts of this essay. The title is in homage to Patrick E. Johnson's '"Quare" Studies, or (Almost) Everything I Know about Queer Studies I Learned from my Grandmother' (2007: 124). However I use 'Quia' rather than 'Quare', as it is closer to my Nigerian heritage in pronunciation. The term 'crip' (short for the derogatory term 'cripple') that has been reclaimed by some disabled people, is used here in solidarity, with respect and in homage to Robert McRuer's *Crip Theory*.

2. *Muhammad Ali and Me* was first staged at Ovalhouse Theatre in 2008, performed by Mojisola Adebayo, Charlie Folorunsho and Jacqui Beckford, directed by Sheron Wray. Revived at Albany Theatre, London in 2016, it is published by Oberon Books in *Mojisola Adebayo: Plays One*.

3. Sebidi, Lebamang J. 'Towards a Definition of African Humanism' in M. Gideon Khabela and Z.C. Mzoneli (eds) *Perspectives on Ubuntu: A Tribute to FEDSEM* (1998) Alice: Lovedale Press: 62.

4. Ukaegbu, V. (2007) 'Grey Silhouettes: Black Queer Theatre on the Post-war British Stage', in Godiwala, D. (ed.) *Alternatives within the Mainstream 2: Queer Theatres in Post-War Britain*. Newcastle: Cambridge Scholars Publishing: 322–338.

5. Okagbue, O. and Igweonu, K. (2014) *Performative Inter-Actions in African Theatre 1: Diaspora Representations and the Interweaving of Cultures*. Newcastle: Cambridge Scholars Publishing: 1-2.

6. Gilroy, P. (1995) '"...to be real": The Dissident Forms of Black Expressive Culture', in Ugwu, C. (ed.) *Let's Get it On: The Politics of Black Performance*. Seattle: Bay Press: 12–33.

For further critical commentary on *I Stand Corrected,* see the interview with me in Caoimhe McAvinchey's *Performance and Community: Commentaries and Case Studies* (2014) and my chapter 'Revolutionary Beauty out of Homophobic Hate: A Reflection on the Performance *I Stand Corrected*' in *Applied Theatre: Aesthetics*. (White, G (ed.) London: Bloomsbury Methuen 2015: 123–155). For a quick visual impression of the live show, see Lisa Fingleton's five-minute short *A Conversation with Mamela Nyamza and Mojisola Adebayo* (https://www.youtube.com/watch? v=qMAwbAp6C1U). For a more extensive insight, see Sue Giovanni's 27-minute film on *I Stand Corrected* http://vimeo.com/80282830. A documentary by Shelley Barry featuring *I Stand Corrected* in its entirety is available at https://www.youtube.com/watch?v=WjjiOutaH9Q

'Jenn': 4 poems

All My Talents

All my talents
Just gold that you can snatch from underneath me
All my talents
Just something you can take from me
All my talents
You, exploiting me
Because I believed, that you believed in me

You left me weak
Physically and mentally
You left me weak
I put my life into your life
I put my heart into your life
I pulled you so far up, you grew tall
And squashed me under your foot

Your intellect masked under the cruelty of insults
You liked me weak
You walked out the door
And left me alone
Bereft of life force
Dragging myself out of bed
I learned to create again
From a new core of life, unleashed
Full on honesty this time I would not retreat
This time, I would become the centre of my world
Money doesn't matter when you have hope and you
believe in yourself.
Without hope you are poor

All my talents

Just gold that you can snatch from underneath me
All my talents
Just something you can take from me
All my talents
You, exploiting me
Because I believed, that you believed in me

But I chose, to wake up
From the sleep of exploitation
I woke up and found my voice
I found my small heart connected to a bigger
expanse
This is what I thought
Stripping the planet to feed our own needs
This is the behaviour we learn, EXPLOITATION
Our selfish, hedonistic lifestyles
Draining the planet of necessary resources

When will we stop this addictive self destructive
behaviour
Earth's talents, earth green, earth life, earth life
force
Which nurtures our talents
The human race – to take, to take, to take from
And keep taking from
To feed our own needs
Not so different to how you treated me!

All my talents
Just gold that you can snatch from underneath me
All my talents
Just something you can take from me
All my talents
You, exploiting me
Because I believed, that you believed in me

Everything starts on a personal level and is fed into
this huge expanse
The microcosm and the macrocosm
When you choose to wake up
You'll really get it
It's like looking at the world under a microscope
It's all connected
When someone exploits you
You exploit someone too
We are all connected

All my talents
Just gold that you can snatch from underneath me
All my talents
Just something you can take from me
All my talents
You, exploiting me
Because I believed, that you believed in me

Between Two Women

This is not my rhythm
This is not my rhyme
This is not the love
That I should feel inside (repeat)

The anger between
Passed abuse still remains
What... are you talking to me this way?
Am I talking your language?
But there is very little understanding.
This is not how it should be
Between (pause) two women

Am I holding your hand
But the distance separates us
Where's the level
Of respect and understanding
Are we just falling into a masculine/
feminine role?
Where is the love?
Where is the strength?
Where is the sensitivity
Between (pause) two women (repeat)
This is not my rhythm
This is not my rhyme
This is not the love
That I should feel inside (repeat)

This is too abrupt
Between (pause) two women
Between (pause) two women
Between (pause) two women

Where is it... the nurturing love, love,

love, love, love, love nurturing love
Are we lessening our womanliness?
What are we afraid of?
Society says it all
Shall we get married then?
Will it show more of our commitment?
Will we be accepted then?
Especially me in my community?

WHO GIVES A FLYING FUCK!!

(pause, breath)

The strength inside our heart to grow
To touch life with love
This is our responsibility
Our only responsibility to the universe
And to be ourselves
To be ourselves
Between, between, between (pause) two
women

Insane

Another human being looking for shelter, shelter
from the storm

If I travel across waters
To another country
Sign a piece of paper and they let me in
Does that make me a migrant, refugee, an asylum
seeker
Or just another human being like you
Another human being looking for shelter, shelter
from the storm

If I am having a challenging day at work
And grey skies seem to be looming
If I call a friend for a chat
Isn't this another kind of shelter
Shelter from the storm
Does that make me a migrant, refugee, an asylum
seeker

Am I not just another human being looking for
shelter, shelter from the storm

Looking for shelter, shelter from the storm
In the warmth of an embrace
From the smile on your face
From the candle that's lit when it's dark to light my
way
From the donation of blankets to keep me warm
From the cup of tea made after a long day at work
Does that make me a migrant, refugee, an asylum
seeker
Am I not just another human being looking for
shelter, shelter from the storm

Separation causes corruption, we do it all the same
Labels
Looking at other as another, another other than me
Yet the other is just another human being
Another human being looking for shelter, shelter
from the storm
Barricades, bars and borders
Laws written down on pieces of paper
Pieces of paper where values are placed
To keep our own space just in case...
FEAR, misguided thoughts
Because the world belongs to everyone
Take off your dark shades you masquerade in day
after day

We are all just looking for shelter, shelter from the
Storm

Like oceans, rivers, streams and seas, that work in
harmony to connect the green, the earth
That connect our roads, our large ships, our trails in
the sky by air
That connect our small boats
How can a piece of paper with a law written down,
hold more value than a life drowned

As human as our being may be
All of us are looking for some kind of shelter,
shelter from the storm

Under The Influence

Under the tidal wave.
I am under the tidal wave.

Passions drifting into the unknown.
Pushing me into subjective desires.
Laughing, laughing.
It is not as though I can stop it right?

I want her
I want her
I want her
Objective life, stand back.

I am finding it hard to, face her face, her smile.
Words won't expand directly, I'm stuttering
Trying to read her mind.
Can she read mine?
Never

All complexities of the imagination
Illusionary desires.
Shut up head.
Take away the visualise, vision.
Take that one out
Take that out.
Be serious, not too serious, interact
I am picturing her naked.

Shut up head... shit.
Think of something else.
I'm trying to have a serious conversation here.
Talk to her, smile and smile and respond.
No it's OK she can't read my mind.
She's walking away... damn...

I panic, I want to grab her arm and say 'don't leave'
Too dramatic I've only just met her.
I want to say 'where are you going, can I come' and skip along beside her
To the yellow brick road.
I want to say 'I WANT YOU'... umm no
Instead I somehow manage to grab her glass and say 'I'll get you another'
Result...
Now she'll have to come back right?
Wow, I mean wow, I mean like... she'll come back right?

Delphine Spencer

Two Worlds That Merge As One

We have been friends for many years, she and I. We have shared many secrets, many thoughts and feelings.

We were inseparable, so much so that we were often one. She was a trusted and loyal friend. As a child growing up within a house where violence was a regular occurrence, and thoughts of death often came knocking on my door, she protected me when I needed her the most. She knew me before I knew me.

If you were to ask me where she is, I can only say: she is not located in my head, not in my stomach, not in my legs or feet, not even in my arms. She is an integral part of my being; she embraces the whole of me. She was my darkness and gave me warmth when I was cold, and understanding when no one else could. She was my companion when I was lonely. She gave me my dreams of a better world.

As I got older I realised that she was also the reason for my reckless behaviour, my mood swings; for my not taking responsibility for my actions, hurting those who showed me warmth and kindness. I decided that I did not want to be her friend any more, and I was happy. She was holding me back; she was causing me problems that had an effect on all areas of my existence. Then I felt free, like an eagle flying gracefully, high in the sky, without a care in the world. I was glad she had gone, never to return.

Without her, life was good – so I thought. I knew deep down that something was missing, but I ignored her. She tried to get my attention, drawing me back to the old ways of thinking, feeling and behaving. But I had years of developing strategies for keeping her at bay, and I was determined to win this game.

I had to admit, though, that it was becoming more difficult, and I was running out of options.

She returned without warning. Like a shadow in the night, like the nightfall that swallows everything in its sight. This time she was different and making a statement, and there was no escaping her. She needed me as much as I needed her. Like a baby needs the womb to grow and develop. To survive.

I realised then that to be truly me I needed to stop running from her, as this would only take me further away from me.

I need to embrace her, not fear her; love her, care for her as she did for me. She needs my understanding, compassion, and support in taking risk. My journey to wholeness is like the seasons; a cycle that is ever-evolving, like trees that need to shed their leaves to make way for new growth. In doing this my darkness and my light can exist together and give me an acceptance of who I really am; two worlds that merge as one.

Olivette Cole-Wilson

Ode to Death

Take me gently, while sitting or sleeping; quietly –
Please take me when I am at peace with my maker, family and
friends.
Take me carefully, when I still have my zest for life and for this
world.
Take me, please, before I lose all sense of reason, self, direction
and reality.
Please grant me time to tie up loose ends, neatly; pack my
boxes and make my home tidy.
Come when my children and grandchildren are at peace with
the world and themselves.
If possible, come when I have that smile of love and content-
ment on my face.
Then, when you come, I will be ready.

Roxanne Simone: 10 poems

Black Rose

I met her in a dream.
Her riotous beauty and unwavering presence held my sadness momentarily as if she knew my pain and had come to create chaos.
Because she also had a knowing that chaos was my bittersweet addiction.
In this exchange I felt so sure of one thing.
That we had met before.
The lines of her face felt familiar.
Like I had swum the depths of them in another distant dream.
Like a black rose, I wanted to admire her beauty layered so precisely and intricately over her dark body.
I had an urge to touch her tears, one by one pulling away petals of the idiosyncratic wonder that united us whilst reciting 'she loves me', 'she loves me not', but I faltered.
I faltered because she was smiling,
Smiling and dividing her light in a million different directions, as if glitter covered the surface of her peculiar face.
And at the height of my awe I was dragged away.
She loves me not. She loves me not.

Mirror Image

Looks weighted down with dirt were thrown and caught by the back end of sour words. It was a toxic hysteria and my mind was searching for the last word; I had to have it.

But right at the point of anger I was met halfway. My eyes darted to an angry bullseye – I was staring into the eyes and mouth of my hate. I was instantly weak but mostly transfixed. Time crawled up to us and tried to interfere. I raised my hand to time and firmly said 'STOP' to which it instantly bowed down with an elegant grace I was unfamiliar with.
As time built a universe around us, I was shaken, slowed down...
The cursing lips before me were blood red, soft, needing, bursting, inviting. Soft dark cheeks that only knew rebellion held a soft smile even through a strong frown. I held out my hands, confusion in my gut, it mustn't rise out and into this vision for it may alter this image.

But too late I cried it out. I cried confusion.

They were small tears, pearl shaped and silver. Very discreet. For in front of me was the most beautiful woman I have ever felt. The backs of her eyes were littered with stars, I counted them until I lost count. I had not anticipated my resentment would melt into thick sweet honey before me. What was I to do? The time that didn't exist was surely running out. Breathing in the sweet scent I saw myself beyond the stars.
I tried to take it all in and I weakened.

Something left my gut, I was lighter.

Something flew from my shoulders, I was taller.

My eyes expanded and the anti light that still existed twisted, spiraled, made beautiful formations in the geometry of life, and beyond.

My hand rose, stopped and rested on the tall neck of this thing,

of beauty, of bitterness, at the fine point between love and hate. The point that celebrated duality and had allowed me to be part of it. For everything I knew I despised, it was everything inside me that was throbbing with love.
Divine love.

And with that, time sliced into our space and there I was and there she stood. Looks weighted down with dirt were thrown and caught by the back end of sour words.

We were in the fight, inching closer to verbally attack. Feeling my defenses rise, I fell, we both literally fell, crashed our tired lips onto each others', and we melted into thick sweet honey together.

I swam slowly but effortlessly further into her. And she reached into me and hate disappeared with our fight. Coming round from this, I rested my head on her. I was tired of fighting the one that I loved with hate. I was weak with relief. I was poor in everything else because the truth, this truth had robbed me of everything that ever existed inside of me.

And I was dragged away screaming. Again

Moments

Silhouetted hourglass:
the rise and fall of her breath.
There's a song being sung but I am way out of my depth.
My heart has wept.
Oh my heart has wept.
Her body is the story I hadn't met yet.
I read her neck-letters trailing down her spine;
There's history and scars that are tending to mine.
The colour, the shapes, the loss on her thigh,
I absorb with my hands, and enhance with my sighs.
I break down into stars, to feel what I see,
timelessly existing in her tender beauty.
She twists into gold.
She twists into gold.
She looks at my chest and honey unfolds.
A hand on my hot cheek is an attack.
An attack I melt into and I won't make it back.

Stop Sign

At times I close my eyes
to see her staring back at me.
I visit passion to arrive at my pain;
I reach into darkness, seduced by her name.
She sank her teeth deep into my skin,
to devour the bone;
bite marks that excite,
bite marks leaving a mess,
bite marks drowned in red
on a greater mess,
sheets twisting into rouge upon the bed.
Red wine clinging to fear,
fear embellished in red wine.
She left me that night,
drinking tears.
Repulsed at my grief,
not holding it in.
Hailing a shiny double decker
she then climbed aboard,
to eye glaze my body,
until she was gone.
I was left in danger,
And I am now dangerous.
Jealous. Same thing.
Of everything.
My eyes glow red in guilt,
tired of reliving his forced-on-me sin.
So yes, I close my eyes
and she stares through me,
I fight time to have her laid next to me,
hands on my chest,
rubbing menthol wax across my breasts;
reaching down lower to heal what's left.
She moves through me,
fires at me;
Orange bullets that kill me, beautiful,
sending me to her heaven lower than my hell,
with poetry that sexed me up,

words in books that make us swell.
She sews up the aftermath
with pearly white teeth that
pin me against walls she built too high for the climb,
but perfect for the chaos;
keeping pieces of my heart inside her space,
not to escape.
I can't breathe in this bliss.
I can't breathe in this.
I desired to fall, unfold into the air,
to stare at the stop signs
and breathe whilst I am there.
She was a warning
And yes I was hurt.
Left longing, throbbing, staggering Central London streets,
fighting off the men that wanted her but were left with me.
I wanted to stay but I saw red. red. red.
I knew to survive him I had to play dead.
My legs were pinned beneath him so my mind ran instead.
But power ran too,
on the night that I almost died
There are two but I can't decide
which one was final.
End of.
Black.
The night I was attacked?
Or the night we ate in joy and in songs we sat,
where her colours danced with their own forgotten dreams;
that nursed me motherly,
tended like a lover,
held me like a father
and kissed me like the end,
that stepped through dreams,
silhouetted upon white walls that she provoked into red.
This was night number two my body tasted death.

Chiaroscuro

People like us.
Like me.
Like you.
We think wild. See wild.
Sleep wild. Dream wild.
Wander wild.
We eat our sacrifices, we clothe ourselves in faith of the unknown.
The stars bring us reassurance, the water whispers knowing and the early morning fog is a hope.
We breathe in stars and breathe out desire.
We drink down numbers that quench our longing to understand what cannot be understood.
We are fighters.
We are art.
We are light, dark. Sharp; chiaroscuro.
We are relentless.
We demand absolutely nothing but seek everything soft, tender, full of pain.
We read between every line, we study the leaves of the trees and ask the soil for answers.
We are obsessed.
Obsessed with what we cannot have because we know deep down in the infinite abyss that we can.
We can.
We just need to see.
And we do.
Eventually.
We see all that we saw and were afraid to see.
And blame time for our bad choices.
We are lovers. And we love.
Simply.
We choose love. We chose this.
We love, love. And we need it wild. Always wild;

to breathe, to wake, to exist, to be here, in this now.
It is rarely safe, almost always uncomfortable and aches to the
edges of forever.
We know this.
And we will still never go for less.

Hourglass

She appeared.
She appeared to have fallen out of my thoughts and into my Eden.
She served me time in a tall hour glass.
It was deliciously nostalgic but aggressively bitter on the tongue.
It softened my sharp edges and held me seductively by the neck.
I was love drunk, sex drunk, past drunk and presently lost in the sight of her body.
Her weakness was my strength, my strength sliced through her decade of regret.
Two less than halves that still made a whole.
And there we were.
Our second chance.
We drank down the time year by year to take us back to purity, and it was there we danced wildly and dangerously, not letting go. Not letting go.
The grey years unfolded into distance and I lost my steps, my foot got caught in the thick mud now beneath us.
Sinking. Fighting. Feeling. Loving. Crying. Reaching. Arms tired, hands slipping, I disappeared.
I disappeared into the mud full cycle.
And now the soil was ready. I emerged, to begin creating the Eden she appeared in
an hour glass of time ago.

Ambush

I do not visit you in your castle full of pain;
As I do not dwell in eagerness to press my lips upon your name.
It's an ambush. Always.
You care not for riot nor angst.
You stir me into green, using her body, standing before me,
eyes that unpeel me.
And we dance, we love, sex, dream, cry, fight, one step, two
step, we are saved, we still fight.
My body gives way because you do that thing you do.
I search and I scream at this thing within me; that uncurls into
you.
Where do you start and where do I stop? – in this time and
deceitful space you cannot be stopped and I cannot stop.
Never with you.
You cover my back, spread across my chest. I catch your tears
and lay us to rest.
A final blow, the darkest goodbye.
I do not enter your castle of pain,
But there you are, ambushing mine.
And I wake. I wake.
Laid in the ache, writhing in pain, holding the dream, exhaling
your name.

Growth

I long for that time again.
That sweet, hot, nurturing time
When the fire would unite us and the water not divide us.
When poetry became the flowers of a dream space we named ours.
That fragment of time where we gazed at fragile vases and witnessed the same blossoming, the same growth, the same colour.
Without a disagreement in sight, quiet mind or soft body.
Where the only fight was against the darkness we both knew would destroy us. Whatever 'us' meant.
You never said you loved me, but the stars revealed your secret whilst the moon speaks of mine every night.

Recovery

Abrupt start, juvenile views, it was white on the playground, only black on the news.

And she was confused.

Yes I was confused.

And so were my peers, who grew tired of class, and would play with my fears.

This was my 'friend', whose words hid within the numerous layers of my delicate skin.

It was my friend who came to tea, sleepovers, shared secrets, clothes and girly magazines who boldly spoke out about what it meant to be me.

I was eight years young, with a younger heart, juvenile views and an abrupt start.

So whilst I was writing in class, doing my work, just as I was asked –

she invited me into a conversation she knew all about: that I was wrong and abnormal, she spoke of the skin I was in.

'You are the wrong colour, look – everyone else is white'

and I looked with my heavy head around the room and realised she was right.

I couldn't argue back because she wasn't telling lies and the hurtful aching truth fell slowly from my eyes.

I've buried it deep but it likes to come up and play out, as vivid as ever; like it happened yesterday.

It's fresh, stubborn and it can't be scrubbed away.

Those words, that phrase – underscored my primary days.

Time can heal and time can serve those in getting what they deserve.

What I deserved I did not get, and my only wish is something that cannot be.

I want to travel through time and hold the young, eight year old me. And squeeze her and wipe her tears and say,

'Things get better,

don't give up your years.
Let it go.
Find strength – YES YOU CAN!'

But a naïve eight year old in a field of white would never understand
...and anyway it got worse, the ridicule: the games and laughs spread onto my afro hair that was pulled back and into a single plait.
They would pull it and say things like 'it looks like a poo.'
I cried and I cried – if only they knew.
The day came when a lady blow dried it straight.
It was light, wispy and I never felt more great, but within an hour of this alien bliss I was crying to my mum with a head full of grit.
Grit that was taken off the road and thrown into my shiny new hair.
I cried into sleep as they laughed into theirs.
Time can heal and time can serve those in getting what they deserve.
What I deserved, I did not get, for my only wish is something that cannot be: I want to bend time and sit with the younger me, hold her hand, stroke her head and warn her of what is up ahead.
For it fell into pain, yes it fell into pain when my all my girl friends grew breasts, it was an entirely new game:

'Roxanne the brown nosed reindeer, had a very flat chest...'

the rumoured jingle of choice one year, nicely confirmed as it was sung in my ear.
And anyway the boys that mastered that genius lyric didn't like black girls as love interests, so it didn't matter that I had a flat chest.
And plus I was the wrong colour and had afro hair; it was white on the playground, only black on the news.

And I was confused. Yes I was confused. And so were my peers,
growing tired of class, would play with my fears.
And it happened again.
And again.
And again.
And I didn't have friends who shared my look, my shape or my
hair so I was really confused, yes really confused.
I fell out with life,
I fell out with girls,
I fell out with boys,
I fell out with teachers and made lots of noise,
I answered them back,
I challenged their notions,
and I've re-lived those moments in painful slow motion.
And I wish I could shout, I wish I could scream at the confused,
lost, adolescent me,

'Apply yourself and get your grade,
grit your teeth,
work through the pain,
don't let these sad lonely years be lived in vain.
Do your bit.
Don't drop the ball,
because something is waiting, it's called "life after school"
which is full of mystery and offers a clean slate.
So stop fighting everyone with your mouthfuls of hate.'

And I scraped on by, yes I scraped on by, with A grades in
English and English Lit – I had something to show from the
years of abyss.
It could of got better – in places it did – and as if time did bend,
I found myself strutting the clubs with my afro hair, the same
boys oh they looked, and the girls also stared.
'Hasn't she blossomed!' rang in my ear. I waltzed around the
place with zero fear.
And then I crashed into an older man.

My heart was the perfect size for his hands.

My body folded up and away into his. I finally had a place to hide, but this was a man who compulsively lied.

I didn't know at first, all I knew, was that I seemed to be enough for him to say, I love you.

So I buried myself in a love that drew blood, when it came to my power – I just didn't have enough to stay on the surface he resurfaced as he twisted my mind.

He hit me, he kicked me and held up a knife.

Time can heal and time can serve those in getting what they deserve.

What I deserved, I did not get, for my only wish is something that can not be, I want to storm through time and sit with the young adult me.

I would thank her for the strength she had in that dark, dark time. I would promise her that there's a time for light. But empty promises it could be perceived initially, I'm twenty nine now and I'm yet to feel free.

But one thing I am is in recovery.

Recovery of the dark means I am one day closer to living in light, and my eight year old self can rest from the fight.

But in the meantime, because time cannot bend, find me giving flowers of forgiveness to myself and those friends.

Grey Area

Black
White
Grey – is where the Black puts her,
Grey – is where the White has put her
No-where – is where the Grey puts her.
She drowns in salty-sour waves of White faces.
Chokes whilst talking articulately – slowly turned south east to the
Black ones. (The faces, oh the faces!)
She sees the intellect of her circumstances, to adapt like a chameleon.
Forever moulding, seductively, wildly – with more colour, hue and saturation than they all collectively could ever dream to dance with, or sleep with... or love... or like.
Lighting up the space and nursing the war wounds of the hopeful concupiscent liars, leaving an aftertaste of vile danger.
Too dangerous to love but safe enough to leave.
She used to control effortlessly...
So tired!
Sick – Because that's the tone of a sick person: Grey.
The Grey area never done anyone any favours.
In the Grey; it's true. No one knows where they stand. Grey has no power.
No validity. It is not one; it is not the other.
So what is it?
They are all intrigued, but aren't they the ones that know best?
...know enough to run their bloodstained, illiterate fingers through – the transfixing mesmerizing, hypnotizing, compelling, gripping, thrilling vision...
That is...
Her hair.
That's all.
Her hair!
But they know.

Because they know that their daughter's friend's cousin's half-brother also has this hair.

So they know. Everything. About her.

Let us not go back to Black. Let us not even start.

It is Hell. Between two worlds. Hell.

But the old White faces will have a go when drink is the only thing left in common with the wife.

And Black will go there. Because they can. Maybe they feel the need to educate on Malcolm X

Like she's never embraced the side of her so unknown. Buried. Denied.

They've assumed she doesn't hear the whispers of her ancestors.

She's one step ahead.

To catch herself before she jumps.

The leader doesn't know – her whiteness blinds the black in her eye.

The affiliates said 'Denial is a river in Egypt'.

And she is left.

Alone.

Knowing that loneliness isn't felt when money is company.

There goes the White.

So let us bring back the Black.

The Black that never embraced her the way she chases 'it'.

Grey will not serve.

And she promised herself

She would jump before she serves herself on a silver platter of conformity.

She knows she is between two worlds.

Please do not remind her.

It is too grey.

And please.

Whoever said their favourite colour was Grey anyway?

Chardine Taylor-Stone

To be Femme: Lesbian Guerrilla Soldier

In the days before *The L Word*, Google and YouTube I found queer culture on the bookshelves of my local library. Often whilst skipping school I would attempt to hover inconspicuously by the Judy Blumes and other books for teenage girls and gradually make my way to the LGBT section. The books I came across were for White people by White people. As a young Black girl it really felt that my queer desires could only be expressed through a prism of Whiteness and White beauty standards. A kind of androgynous, floppy-haired waistcoat and T-shirt chic that to my working class and West Indian sensibilities didn't quite fit. I needed colour, accessories, nail extensions and yes, even a bit of bling. When *The L Word* eventually came about, still it wasn't quite right. Smearing someone else's lipstick in a passionate embrace didn't really appeal to me, the energy just wasn't there. So I closed the books and switched channels in the same way I switched off my emotions. It's only now that I look back and I wonder whether if I had seen any representation of strong and proud Femmes of colour I could have skipped those depressing years of being in relationships with unthreatening and soft cis-men.

In *Baby, You are My Religion*, a study of pre-Stonewall lesbian bar culture by Marie Cartier, she describes a Femme as a 'decidedly feminine woman who openly valued masculinity within a female biology'. Who a Femme desired was key to her identity, and like Cartier's description, my journey towards becoming Femme is very much tied to my desire for masculinity in the form that she describes. In Feminist circles we talk about how naming our oppression is the first step towards our liberation. However as soon I was able to name my experiences and desires under this term it looks set to be erased and replaced with something very different. In our age of postmodern Queer Theory, Femme has become shorthand for 'feminine', and so anything from wearing lipstick to a dash of glitter on your cheekbones now gets hashtagged *#Femme*. Its role as a descriptor for a queer woman's desire has been slung aside. Recently, an article from the website *Everyday Feminism*, titled '4 Ways to Support Queer Femmes - Instead of Erasing Us from Queer Communities', was shared in my Facebook newsfeed. Along with a perky cartoon of different types of Queer Femme it claimed that cis men could also claim the identity. I found the article galling. Femme was not created in a vacuum. It was born in the bar culture of working class lesbians, especially women of colour. It was nurtured by women who suffered homophobia in ways which I am grateful that I don't have to experience today. We should respect those who fought for Femme to be recognised as a label of pride; it is because of their resistance that Femme and femininity is now considered radical in queer spaces. Remember that when applying your lipstick for an Instagram selfie.

Too often terms that have been created by lesbian women to describe their lived experience are viewed as immaterial, and so easily consumable to all. We are misogynistically told that 'terms evolve' so we must accept that cis men and straight women can attach the term to themselves and not only that, be grateful for their inclusion. Would we allow this for anything else? Femme has a history, let's be mindful of not erasing it in our mission to queer all things.

We cannot escape the irony that Lesbian Feminists and Queer Feminists, often at war with each other on Twitter, both share similar snobbish views towards the Butch and Femme dynamic. Some of this attitude is a form of Queer classism: we have yet to be 'liberated' from our binary mindset by academic theory. Mistrust towards Femmes who are cisgendered women is that we have the privilege of passing as straight. This cannot be denied; I can move through the world with an ease that those who present differently cannot. The flipside of this is that I am also invisible to those in my community. But Femmes are a resourceful lot, and the Femme cue towards a Butch that Kate Bornstein describes as 'hot fun' is its own highly sophisticated calling signal. The trick is to 'meet them in the eyes, glance quickly away, then slowly look back into the butch's eyes and hold that gaze'. In another era we were known to stand seductively next to the jukebox whilst glancing and then knowingly selecting the right record. A coded invitation to be asked to dance. There are ways, and then there are Femme ways.

This resourcefulness has also meant that Femmes used their privilege to get work to support their Butch partners who couldn't find employment. They are the ones who bravely out themselves when they held the hands of their partners in public, constantly destroying society's notion of what a queer woman looks like and whom she chooses to love.

So why do I see the separation of desire from the Femme identity as a worrying form of erasure? For my queerness to be acceptable to the straight world I'm expected to desire what patriarchy deems desirable in women, femininity. A Femme's desire for a Butch or Stud is therefore a radical one because society tells us every day that those bodies are undesirable. Dismiss it as binary, but I am a Femme who desires and loves Butches. I will not deny that for the sake of fashion, for acceptance, or even for Queer credibility. All of us as women, and particularly as queer women of colour whose sexuality has been owned and colonised for so long, must take pride in who we desire, especially if that desire is considered deviant from the norm. It is for these reasons that I am very vocal and somewhat protective about how the term Femme has come to be used today.

It took me awhile to find Femme, it took heartbreak and a display of solidarity which I will never forget. As someone said to me recently, Femme is such a bonding identity, and those bonds kept them alive. This Femme proudly struts in the heels of those who went before her. Glamorous guerilla soldiers, warrior queens and rebels, each and every one.

Mica Hamilton: 4 poems

Stay Woke

Eyelids lowered
You bite the side of your lip as you saunter over
Looking down at me
With hunger
Sliding the hair out of your face
And looking me up and down
As if I were a five star main course
Placing your hands on my waist
Your hips lead me to the beat of the music
That has us in a trance
Flexing my hips towards you
As you pull yourself in closer
So close I can smell your desires
You place your lips on my neck
Gently kissing the spot that sends me in a tail spin
With those lips
Brown and enveloping
Feeling every curve and muscle in those lips deep inside
You draw back and leave me wanting
Returning your stance and staring straight through me
In one fluid movement you sink your teeth in before I can catch
    my breath
Instantly lighting my cunt on fire
Soaking me

Darkness descends as you restrain me
Grabbing me by the hair and kissing me on the mouth deeper
than you had before
Deep enough to fade away all sense of pain and pleasure
Your tongue finds places in me that no one else ever could
Places I didn't know existed
Watching your biceps flex as you lift me up on to the counter
    with ease
The only arms that have the strength to fuck me
The way I need to be fucked
Grabbing my face with all the passion you've suppressed
Craving me
Unable to control yourself
Sliding your hands underneath my top
Paralysing me with your touch
Feeling for my chest
And tearing my bra down
To reveal what you've been dreaming of
Teasing my nipples with your finger tips
My legs hooked over your shoulders
Feeling your shoulder blades tighten with every movement
Biting your bottom lip I feel myself flood
As you reach your hand under my skirt
And find her.

Frangelico

Skin like hazelnut
Caramel when sun rays catch you
Smooth, as you pour down my throat.
I find myself savouring the taste on my lips not wanting it to
    end.
Unable to recall a time when my taste buds sparked every other
    sense in my body this way
Swirling my tongue around searching for every last drop
Warmth spreads outwards hitting every synapse on the way
A thousand shades of brown remind me of a time I've yet to
    experience
You are 40% sugar
With a dash of vanilla and lashings of cocoa.
Steeped in the spirits of all the Goddesses gone before us.
Pour me another
I want to feel all of those shades of brown
Touch every nerve as you flow through me
Heating me up like the sun
Your viscosity.
Just the right amount of **thick**
Crafted a hundred years ago by those I've never met.
For this moment
As I part my lips
And close my eyes
Tilt my head back
And let you enter me.

Frangelico

Hot Fucking Chocolate

We are hot.
Fucking.
Chocolate.
Do we go for the instant type, quick, just add liquid and heat
Perhaps cream?

Or maybe even home style
Simmering chocolate with cinnamon
Nutmeg
And vanilla
Bringing it to the boil
Waiting aeons
For you to be ready
Serving it in my favourite cup
Watching all the spice rise to the top
As lips part
And all that smooth, thick chocolate enters my mouth

You're still too hot.

Take it slowly
I'm not quite ready
To experience this
Hot
Fucking
Chocolate

This hot fucking chocolate
That took years
To grow.
A simple pod

Protected by an outer shell
That must be cracked open
And tended to delicately
With precision
And years of knowledge.
In order to reveal the smooth brown
That we can now call chocolate
Your name used to be cocoa
But I've turned you into something else.
Patiently waiting years.
For this moment.
Sprinkles of brown sugar
Melt and swirl into you
As I prepare myself for the final moment.
I'm coming for you
My hot
Fucking
Chocolate.

Lovers Rock

I want to get high with you and listen to the bass line
As we watch the smoke curl above our shadows and let the
    sweat drip off us
Fingertips trace down the nape of my neck
As my spine curves and my back arches
Feeling your tongue slide inside me
Making my legs spread as wide as they can
Toes stretched and reaching for the stars

Looking down on your heart shaped mouth
And watching your head disappear between my thighs and re-
    emerge with wet lips
Your physique
Perfectly bent
Creating lines I could only dream of
Hair tickling my thighs as you crawl back to your knees
Staring up at me with those eyes
Those eyes that make me melt with their intensity and depth
Giving me trench foot
And I fall deeper and deeper into them

The bass rumbles from the speakers
Mirroring my short breaths
Making me dizzy
You're intoxicating
Putting me under your spell
And your tone of voice is the only thing my cunt needs to hear
Half a bottle of lube used up in a week
Solo play and my thoughts are no longer enough
I'm breathing you in
Soaking up your essence

I stare at you sat on top of me
Feeling your hair behind my ears
Touching my favourite spot
Feeling your pelvic bone against mine
Flexing towards me as I open myself for you
I'm craving your fingertips
Your hands
Your legs
Your upper inner thighs
And beyond
As the electricity lights me up from the inside
Take me to a higher power
Iridescent

Staring straight into your eyes
And seeing myself reflected
Hearing you sing your orgasm straight into my ears
Whilst you fuck me from behind
Leaning into me
And dragging your lips down my neck
As you hit the spot
That not everyone can reach
But your fingers have the length
And the dexterity
To find the place where my dreams lay dormant
Waiting to be woken

Reaching the apex
I begin to realise that resistance is futile
Surrendering control over to you
And submitting completely
I am taken by you

Kayza Rose

When is the right time?

When is the right time to tell children you're same gender loving (SGL)?

I mean, children don't come with a manual; there are no guidelines. What would their reaction be? Would they understand? Would they... hate you? Have you been open enough – or too open – with them? Will they want to leave your household if you tell them? What if they hate you, are disgusted, or so embarrassed they can't look at you? These were some of the things that went through my mind when it came to the time I thought was best to tell my children I was SGL.

Why did I think this, why did I have all these worries?

I never saw any examples of what to do or how to behave around this subject. What I have seen in society and in my community is that SGL is something you need to be cured of. Something that isn't good, something to be ashamed of. I'm not saying this is typical for all people of my generation or my culture, just that it's my lived experience, and my experience was never positive around being known as SGL. The people that did 'come out' were either teased, shunned or attacked. There was this same message in some of the music I grew up listening to. Half my family is Jamaican and a quarter of it is Cameroonian, both places where being SGL is illegal. Places where SGL individuals are often severely beaten and sometimes killed. This means that many people are living in secret and in shame, never sharing that part of their lives with their family out of fear. Some of these people marry people they aren't attracted to and don't love because they're too afraid to show their true selves. They go on to have children with these people and live in misery.

Young people of today have the internet. We didn't have that when I was growing up. I didn't have access to people who felt like I felt. I didn't have forums I could go to and see healthy examples of SGL couples with children, or read statistics showing how well children of SGL couples did. At one point I really thought I was the only one; that there was something wrong with me because I was different. The fact that I grew up only seeing heterosexual people with children had a profound effect on what I thought 'normal' was.

Before I forget... You must be wondering what happened with my children, right? Well, I told them when they were ten years old. Yes, they're twins LOL. The firstborn took it really well. He said, 'Mum... as long as you are happy then I'm happy, and anyway it's none of my business.' Twin Two didn't like the idea of having an SGL mother; he worried about being 'normal' and what people would think. But we talked it through and within a week he was okay with it.

The twins are now twenty years old. These days they ask me for advice about women and always think I'm dating any pretty female I'm around. We talk about relationships and what we find attractive in a woman. I'd say it worked out quite well for us.

I do hope we will come to a time where 'coming out' isn't needed, and that being SGL will be one of the norms of society. We still have a long way to go... but I do hope!

Olivette Cole-Wilson

Reflections (of an older Black Lesbian)

When I first ventured into the world of politics, Women, Feminism, Pan-Africanism and Black Power thirty-five plus years ago, London seemed to be a hotbed of political activity; I can still recall the excitement of being in a room filled with dynamic Black Women determined to transform the world.

Exploration deepened when I stumbled across a notice for a feminist conference, which I eagerly attended. There I came across radical feminists, revolutionary feminists and Marxist feminists, as well as lesbians of all different shapes, sizes and colours; political lesbians, celibate lesbians, and what I later came to understand as 'butch' and 'femme' lesbians.

Following the conference, and having met up with other black women, we formed a consciousness-raising group. I immersed myself in various feminist activities, from helping out at A Woman's Place, Xeroxing *The London Women's Liberation Newsletter*, to stuffing envelopes at the Outwrite office at Oxford House in Bethnal Green.

The Black Lesbian Group was another organization I was involved in where I met lesbians of all different shades and ethnicities – 'black' in those times was the political term used for all minority ethnic groups of colour: it was all about self-identification and self-definition.

That era, from the mid-seventies to the mid-eighties, was a hive of political activity, with women's groups, activities, actions, protests and marches taking place, throughout the UK, but mainly in London. Centres sprang up; the London Women's Centre, the Brixton Black Women's Centre and the London Lesbian and Gay Centre, to name but a few.

Coming out was something that was hotly debated, not so much because of embarrassment or shame but because it often felt like an onerous and never-ending task: work, school, GP, family, friends, colleagues – though not everyone at once; rather like drip-feeding. Then annoyance would creep in: why? Why do I/we have to justify our very existence? ...and of course there were accounts of work colleagues refusing to talk to known lesbians, and people receiving negative responses from church.

We had debates about Blackness – differing shades, countries of birth, and how 'black' someone was, depending on a spurious list of criteria. Not to mention debates about hair; natural, plaited, straightened, wigs, and what these styles represented. Interestingly, thirty-five plus years on many of the discussions and debates we had then are being had again, and are frighteningly similar in tone, and as poignant now as they were then.

Technology and social media have replaced publications such as *Spare Rib*, *The London Women's Newsletter*, and the multifaceted debates that took place in them, as well as the innovative newspaper *Outwrite*. No more Theatre of Black Women or Sheba feminist publishers bringing us the writings of our Black Lesbian Sisters from across the pond as well as in the UK.

Change is inevitable, but it is important that our visibility, our voices, our passion and our politics do not get lost, marginalized, or written out of history.

P.J. Samuels

Tips for Relating to a Melaninrich Person at a Social Event – that is, Me

~ Alert! Human in the house. Act human.

~ I do not wish to hi-five you because your Dutch courage suggests you should perform for your mates walking behind you. I'm not a mascot.

~ Gate person: I appreciate the rather effusive greeting I was singled out for but I didn't wander in by mistake. I don't need to be reassured it's okay to attend this event I booked tickets for 6 months ago.

~ I do not feel like smiling.

~ Do not attempt to randomly wander through the middle of me and my friends when there is ample space to walk around us. I will block your way and utterly ignore any attempt you make to vocalise/communicate. Including apologies and smiles. I will treat you as invisible as your action rendered me/us. Just be gone.

~ I am fabulous. I know. I woke up that way. Not exotic. Not costumed. Not your sister or your mama working it.

~ Don't attempt to gyrate hard because I smile in your dancing direction. I am not the ultimate authority judging urban dance moves. You don't need to impress me. You are not creating kinship in some language of the waistlines. Just smile back. Or ignore me.

~ Do I need to get a T-shirt that says I am not in a petting zoo?

~ The fact that you don't understand when I speak is an indictment on your education system and your participation therein. Not a function of my melanin. Or accent. Or language. Or 'exoticism'…

~ Just be yourself. Unless you're Racist. Sexist. Homophobic. Misogynist. Judgemental. Assumist – or any combination thereof . Then don't be yourself. Act human.

~You're welcome.

Sokari Ekine

Love in the Age [of] Evolution

This is a story of falling in love at 67. Let's say her name is V...
A mutual friend had introduced us by email in 2014, but apart
from an initial response I had not communicated with her.

After 25 years in London, in 2010 I moved to the US, and
since then have divided my time between southern Florida and
Haiti. New York was a brief respite before I returned for a few
months' work in Haiti. I remembered V... and thought to let her
know I was going to be in the city for a few days over the
holidays. Fortunately she responded, and we set up a lunch
date for 2nd January.

The big decision was what to wear – skirt or pants. I ended
up with the skirt, to give me a more femme, softer look. I had of
course looked up photos of V... as you do in the age of Google
and saw she was a mascufemme, which is pretty much the
same as me. I liked that flexibility, that freedom to twist and
turn.

I was a little apprehensive: she is a name, and I had intellectual anxiety. To help me get past this, and as a genuine desire
to gift, I brought with me a 10"x8" photograph from my *Spirit
Desire* series. It was a flirtatious gesture but I would try hard to
make it seem otherwise.

We had arranged to meet at the Schomburg Center for Re-
search in Black Culture in Harlem. I arrived early and took a
seat outside the Center's small exhibition gallery and waited a
while, looking around.

I had visited the Schomburg a couple of days earlier for the
exhibition *Unveiling Visions: The Alchemy of the Black
Imagination*[1]. Thinking back to the exhibition, it crossed my
mind that Black people have deployed 'imagination' as a way of
surviving what Christian Sharpe calls the 'singularity of anti-
Blackness'[2]. Black Queer Love has also required our imagining
of the possible.

After a while I stood up, thinking to go in and walk around
the gallery again, and suddenly our eyes met. She inside, me

outside, looking in. She was shorter than I expected, and wearing a huge and enveloping black fake-fur winter coat. We both smiled and then exploded into laughter, covering up our first-contact 'check her out' moment. It was a mild, sunny winter day and we decided to walk to the restaurant of her choosing. I can't remember what we talked about but there were no silences. I had this fresh open light feeling, flush, and very much in the presence of the moment.

We arrived at the Sapphire, a Senegalese restaurant. I could see her checking me out as we flirted with subtle looks and well-chosen words, through laughter, and accompanied by the stimulating taste of good food. With a swag encouraged by the moment I brought out what I hoped would be the knockout move of the day, my beautiful black and white photograph of two Haitian women embracing during a ceremonial dance. The photo was one of many I had taken during the annual ten-day ceremonies to mark the founding of Lakou Badjo in the historic Haitian city of Gonaïves. This particular ceremony was in honour of the lwa (spirit) Ogou, who is the patron of the Lakou; I made the photo amidst the many simultaneous 'mountings' (possessions) brought on by dance, drums, song, and the sweet pungent smell of Florida Water cologne; these were moments of intense love and freedom, and appropriate as a gift to a queer black sister.

She was bowled over, delighted, surprised: her eyes were bright, the gap between her teeth almost exploding as she smiled at the deliciousness of the gift.

A few days later I left New York for Washington DC, for a brief visit with friends. I had texted her to say thanks and emailed a couple of promised links but otherwise done nothing. Once on the bus I sent a message saying I was on my way to DC. This became the precursor to three days of flirtatious texting. I found her saucy, intensely sexual, her voice caressing; and she has this huge laugh that passes through and shakes her whole body. Over those three days we talked about everything; we seduced each other with words, with intellect and humour.

By the time I was back in Florida I knew I had to think about whether this was a possibility. I had to think of how love would look for two black, queer and evolving artists. How would we create the space and mindfulness that I so deeply needed, but had failed to find up till this moment? What would a Queer Black Imagination around Love, Art and Struggle look like?

There was no way that I would consider entering into anything but a 'grown up' partnership – no quarrels, willful misunderstandings, games that hurt, pouting silences. Partnership was not the word I was looking for. It would take our coming together to discover that 'lovership' was the word we had created; our word. And we soon came together, for a weekend in Florida. As the time neared my anxiety reached manic proportions. Initially she had wanted to stay in a hotel but these turned out to be too expensive so I suggested she stay with me – no get out clause included! I spent days cleaning the house, preparing food, buying flowers and drinking shots of rum to calm my nerves. To our credit everything went well, except that three hours after her arrival I felt the beginnings of back spasms. These are generally brought on by driving, standing too long, or anxiety and tension, so it wasn't a surprise to me that I ended up with back pain before we had even had a chance to see what might happen. By the next morning the spasms had become unbearable, and I had to resort to a narcotic mix of painkillers and muscle relaxants which knocked me out for 24 hours.

V... was amazing. Looking after my needs and taking care of her own, she fed herself and passed the day reading. By Saturday morning my back had eased a little, and we were able to spend time getting to know each other before she left early on Sunday; the following day I left for two months in Haiti. Although that sounds a bad way to begin, it turned out to be a blessing, as it allowed us to know each other slowly, our relationship evolving over good morning and goodnight conversations. One of the first decisions we made was to recognise the importance of starting and ending our days together, even if only a brief text was possible. This practice, which remains with us today, was crucial during this period of long-distance love – something that neither of us had declared, though its presence was already there.

The declaration or the admission came some months after our initial brunch date. We had arranged that when my Haiti work was finished, instead of returning direct to Florida, I would visit her in NY for around two weeks. We had by this time worked ourselves up into a state of nervous anticipation, wondering how we would manage being in an intimate space together for more than three days, being as we were both in a state of evolution as a couple and set in our ways as separate individuals. Little foibles could become large irritations once in close and sustained physical proximity. How would we manage this? How would we manage intimacy? What does intimacy mean?

Intimacy came to mean multiple forms and levels of erotica. Sexual desire and pleasure were and remain central to our lovership. This we intensified through the 'convergence of the epicurean and sexual desire'[3] – the preparation and consumption of provocative food, the sipping of wine, sometimes fine, sometimes coarse, and yes, occasionally champagne. Arousing our taste-buds as we aroused the nerves that set our skins tingling through sucking, munching, and licking.

Through our creativity; through everyday micro-acts such as working out together at the gym; through shopping for food we would share and taste and relish together; through conversations where we would push each other to think, ideas came and grew and grew. Living with her need for order, and my comfort with disorder, also became part of the erotics of our intimacy. Our lovership took on a life of multiple desires and joy. There were hurdles, of course – not many, but they came, and left us feeling an unwelcome tenderness, as of a bruise. These presented the challenge of being grown up or not. We made the decision at the first hurdle to talk our way through the tender moments rather than leave them to simmer, stew, boil over. We chose to practice being mindful. We chose to write down our own lovership manifesto and to return to this regularly. We chose to love each other, and to understand what exactly loving each other meant and required.

We love, and part of that love is not accepting the monotony of normative language but instead inventing our own language. We love to name objects, events, ways of being. This is what black queer and evolving love does: it pushes language so language is radicalized by queerness, always pushing the boundaries of what and who we are. What is queer is the question we constantly ask, rather than who is queer. And that includes being an evolving person.

Age is seen as a dis/ability. An in/ability or unwillingness to participate in the erotics and desires required for living to the full. In the normative world age is death prefigured and is riddled with social taboos on loving, sexual desire. We, as queer Black women, reject these, and instead we move forward in time by evolving rather than 'aging'.

Notes:

1. https://www.nypl.org/events/exhibitions/unveiling-visions
2. Christina Sharpe "In the Wake: On Blackness and Being, Duke University Press, 2016
3. Marilyn Minter "Food Porn" series, Brooklyn Museum, January 2017

I am what I am
What I am needs no explanation
Wait!
I need to come out...
I am a Christian.
I mean,
I am a woman.
I mean,
I am Rastafarian,
I mean,
I am Jamaican.
I mean,
I am human.
I cannot get my head around this coming out...
I mean...
I AM...

P.J. Samuels

Contributors

Mojisola Adebayo is a performer, playwright, director, producer, facilitator and lecturer at Queen Mary, University of London. She has worked internationally in theatre, television and radio for twenty-five years, from Antarctica to Zimbabwe. Her productions include *Moj of the Antarctic: An African Odyssey* (Lyric Hammersmith), *Muhammad Ali and Me* (Ovalhouse) and *I Stand Corrected* (Artscape, Cape Town). Publications include *Mojisola Adebayo: Plays One* (Oberon), '48 Minutes for Palestine' in *Theatre in Pieces* (Methuen) and the co-written *Theatre for Development Handbook* (Pan). Her PhD thesis is entitled *Afriquia Theatre: Creating Black Queer Ubuntu Through Performance*. Mojisola is currently compiling *Plays Two* and working on her next production, *STARS*. See www.mojisolaadebayo.com for more!

Gray Akotey is a web creative and barber from London now living in Amsterdam. Moving for love that didn't work out, she's decided to stay and experience life in a new city. She is a passionate advocate for visibility among the Black British LGBT+ community and volunteers her time in projects that continue to support that vision.

Roxene Anderson was born and bred in Sheffield, South Yorkshire, where her grandparents settled after crossing the Atlantic from Jamaica in the *Windrush* era. She has a passion for creative arts, and that developed into a love for photography. Now a professional photographer, she resides in Brixton, London. She draws inspiration from her own cultural and sexual identity, creating art which represents those communities in an authentic and positive way. Her mission is to pursue a journey which gives a platform to traditionally marginalised communities, with the power to change the narrative away from the media-saturated stereotypes that currently exist. Roxene is delighted to have her writing acknowledged, and to see it published in a book with an ethos which aligns with these core values.

www.roxene-anderson.com // @roxeneandersonphotography

Eileen Bellot's work is inspired by the world around us, her artwork, nature, dreams, self-exploration, fables and ritual. She uses the written word, storytelling and performance to create work that encourages audiences to pose questions, challenge limiting beliefs, and revere the beauty and magic within the world around us. She creates work that engages new audiences, imbues wonderment and helps to promote commonality and connection. Eileen is currently working on her first play, exploring the tension between women's mid-life transition and whether there is still a place for women's rites of passage in our modern world. Email: questlife@questlife.co.uk; Twitter: @Questlife2; Facebook: Questlife

Doreene Blackstock treads boards for a living. She is a professional actor with over twenty-five years' experience, from Edinburgh Fridge to large-scale RSC, television, radio and film productions; story-telling in all its many theatrical forms is one of her passions. She wrote and performed her one woman show *Behind God's Back* in 2013, and is currently performing in the 5* production of *Much Ado About Nothing* at Shakespeare's Globe Theatre, London.

She wrote 'The Missing I in You' during the devastating break-up of her 18-year relationship with another woman – which on reflection, she now says, was the best gift life could have given her, as the loss forced her to grow beyond her comfort zones, which lead to her becoming, not only a better mother but a much better human being, for which she is truly #Grateful!

Andreena Bogle-Walton is a 36-year-old outspoken lesbian of substance who has many strings to her bow. She works for the NHS as a Smoking Cessation Specialist helping smokers to quit smoking, and specializes in behaviour change. She has been writing honest poetry as a hobby since February 2014 and founded Poetry LGBT Open Mic Night for the LGBT+ community in January 2015.

Poetry LGBT is held in North and South London on the 1st

and 3ʳᵈ Sundays of every month, and is a much-needed social space for creativity and expression. Details of the event can be found on Facebook, Instagram and Twitter @PoetryLGBT or email poetryloungelgbt@hotmail.com.

Kesiena Boom was born in East London in 1994. She is a mixed-race, Black, lesbian feminist writer. Her work covers topics of sexuality, relationships, race and gender. She is also an award-winning sociologist and is working towards a Master's in Gender Studies. Read her collected essays at: kesiena boom.com.

babirye bukilwa, formerly known as Vanessa Babirye, is a multifaceted artist. She is one half of the hilarious international hit *ackee and saltfish*, made for YouTube and then bought by the BBC. Acting professionally since the age of sixteen, babirye already has extensive experience in stage, screen and radio, with her credits including the BBC, Channel 4, the Royal Court Theatre, Hampstead Theatre, and the National Theatre. Also a singer, a poet, and co-founding and co-hosting and managing her podcast turned radio show *Sistren*, babirye has now added playwright to her list. Staying true to the hyper honest ethic and tone of her work, babirye writes mostly biographical pieces and these are her first collections. babirye is a force, taking the word artist and making it her own.

Clementine Ewokolo Burnley writes, works as an organiser in communities of colour, and meditates. Born in Cameroon, raised in Cameroon and the UK, Clementine now lives and writes between lots of different places. You can find her at https://about.me/clementine.ewokolo.burnley or on Twitter at @decolonialheart.

Olivette Cole-Wilson was born in Parsons Green, the fourth of seven children. Her father was a Clergyman and her mother, a Midwife. Her father took up a position as an assistant vicar in East London, the family moved and she has remained there ever since.

Olivette trained as a music teacher, taught at a secondary school then moved into social work, training and counselling.

Qualifications include a Masters in Social Work, a certificate in Counselling and Groupwork, and a Diploma in Black Therapy; she has a private practice in East London.

Having always been passionate about the arts, in particular music, writing and theatre, in her 'prime' Olivette trained to become an actress, and embraces every opportunity to perform.

Olivette was a founder member of Black Womantalk, a collective that published two anthologies of writings by predominantly British Black women; she is also a founder member of Stonewall.

Jennifer Daley is a British actor of dual heritage. Raised in West Yorkshire, she has lived in London since the age of eighteen and has worked in theatre, film and television, with a particular focus on politically-informed original work. She featured in the groundbreaking film *FIT* by Rikki Beadle-Blair, produced by the charity Stonewall, which tackles homophobia within secondary schools. She has also worked in commercial West End theatre and features regularly on BBC Radio 4.

Yrsa Daley-Ward is a writer and poet of mixed West Indian and West African heritage. Born to a Jamaican mother and a Nigerian father, Yrsa was raised by her devout Seventh Day Adventist grandparents in the small town of Chorley in the North of England. Her poetry collection *bone*, is published by Penguin books (2017).

Sokari Ekine is a Nigerian-British writer and visual scholar who has lived and worked internationally in Africa, Europe, Haiti and the US.

Her most recent work, situated in Haiti and Kenya, focuses on African Spiritual Practices as sites of resistance, decolonization, queerness and community. Her personal blogs are: www.blacklooks.org and www.sokariekine.me.

Christina Fonthes is a Congolese-British writer. Her work, laden with themes of womanhood and sexuality, has featured in several publications around the world, including *Ake Review* in Nigeria. Her mantra, 'telling stories through any means possible', allows her to bring untold stories to life through writing, performance, and digital art. Currently based in London, Christina is a member of the writer's collectives Malika's Poetry Kitchen, founded by poet Malika Booker; and Women in The Spotlight, run by Cultureword Commonword. Website: christinafonthes.com.

Joy Gharoro-Akpojotor is a Nigerian-born writer. She writes plays and screenplays. She loves astrology and stories that challenge our perceptions of what reality is! When not writing, she also produces films.

Remi Graves is a London based poet and drummer. A Barbican Young Poet Alumnus, her work can be found in publications such as *Skin Deep*, *Ver Poets Anthology* and *NON Quarterly*. She has performed at Roundhouse, Lovebox, Camp Bestival and Jaw Dance amongst others. Her past projects include a residency at Croydon Library with Spine Festival, and she most recently held the role of Digital Poet in Residence with 1215.today and The Poetry School. Remi is also one half of Gertrude and Jemima, a poetry and music duo, with South African poet and performer Toni Stuart.

Rue Gumbochuma is a poet and songwriter who uses poetry and music to explore the human condition. She aims to create art that challenges societal ideals with themes that usually focus on relationships and religion. Her most recent project saw her exploring culture and identity within the African Diaspora. In the past she has worked with different arts organisations such as Apples & snakes, Vocals & Verses and Beatfreeks to name a few.

Mica Hamilton. Born and bred in Latimer Road, West London, Mica has been inspired by her exciting surroundings, creating and writing about everything and anything that came her way. Passionate about her communities, she is a youth worker, music blogger and crafter. The daughter of a Lovers Rock/Soca DJ and a librarian, her passion for music often moves her to write anything from poetry to fetish porn. You can read her music blog here: www.retrogradeinversion.co.uk.

'Jenn'. I am so very excited to be a part of *Sista!* A little about me: *(Whispering)* Oi tell everyone, I've always loved poetry, the first poem I committed to memory is called *The Night Will Never Stay (*age 12). I remember when I was younger borrowing poetry books from school and accidentally forgetting to give them back ☺ (age 8 or 9). I didn't actually realize how much I love poetry and writing until the opportunity arose to send something in for *Sista*! I discovered I have a wealth of poems, prose... oh, and songs I have written, stored in folders in my home. So, on discovering this, I made a little promise, a pact with the universe... I will continue sharing my poetry, prose and songs, you know, leave a little legacy, my contribution to the world. And so here I am...

Germaine Joseph. I'd say I'm currently a student, studying mental health nursing, and I write for pleasure in my spare time.

Dr Valerie Mason-John M.A. (hon.doc) is the co-author and editor for the first two books to document the lives of Black and Asian Lesbians in Britain. Once named as one of Britain's Black Gay Icons, she was the artistic director of Pride and Mardi Gras Arts Festival. Since retiring from the Queer scene, she is the author of 8 books, including her award-winning novel, *Borrowed Body*, twice award-winning book *Eight Step Recovery - Using The Buddha's teachings to Overcome Addiction*, and twice award-winning book *The Great Black North, Contemporary African Canadian Poetry*. She works as an inspirational Public Speaker, and is one of the leading African Descent Voices in Addiction and Mindfulness. She tours internationally. www.valeriemason-john.com.

Tamara McFarlane. I co-wrote my first play, *Now We Are Here*, which was first shown at Latitude Festival 2016, and then at the Young Vic Theatre. This led to me being commissioned by the Young Vic to write my first full-length play, which I have done, and am working on fine-tuning, and which will be on at the Young Vic sometime in the near future. I am also a poet and have written many poems, a few of which can be found at www.poetrypoem.com/tammy – click on the poem *Always You* to get the full list. I do open mic performances and enjoy poetry immensely. Though none of my post-2014 poems are on this page, I am hoping to put together a bunch of my new poems and get them out there very soon. My agent is Kirsten Foster at Casarotto Ramsay & Associates, and I am on twitter – @taramarayana, and on Instagram where I share poems from time to time @tammyt_leo. You can also find me under my name on Facebook. At the moment I am writing a lot. A poem a day keeps me sane. My great grandmother is my hero, and I strongly believe that, with life, all things are possible – just keep believing.

Phyll Opoku-Gyimah is co-founder and executive director of UK Black Pride. A tireless activist, she sits on the TUC race relations committee and is a trustee of LGBT rights charity Stonewall. In 2016 she made headlines for refusing an MBE, saying, 'As a trade unionist, a working class girl, and an out black African lesbian... I don't believe in empire. I don't believe in, and actively resist, colonialism and its toxic and enduring legacy in the Commonwealth, where – among many other injustices – LGBTQI people are still being persecuted, tortured and even killed because of sodomy laws... that were put in place by British imperialists. I'm honoured and grateful, but I have to say no thank you.' British of Ghanaian descent, Phyll was born in Islington and lived on Woodbury Down Estate with her family, then moved to the countryside, and in the late 80s moved back to London. She is a mother, has a regular column in *Diva* magazine, and works for Public and Commercial Services Union as the Head of Political Campaigns & Equality.

Lettie Precious, born October 1986, is a Zimbabwean-British writer from Sheffield. In 2013 Lettie Precious looked at their boss after a twelve-hour nursing shift in a busy London ward and said, 'See this face, sister? Memorise it because you'll never see it again.' Jobless and on the verge of homelessness, they decided to pursue their passions in the creative arts. In 2016 their writing was notice by one of London's most prolific writer/director/producers, Rikki Beadle-Blair, who gave them an opportunity to be part of his writing festival in partnership with the Theatre Royal Strafford East. In 2017 they were awarded a residency at Arcola Theatre and worked in partnership with the Arts Council to develop their work. Lettie Precious continues to pursue their writing and other creative endeavours.

They can be reached via e-mail: l.precious@hotmail.com or twitter @LettiePrecious.

Kayza Rose is an Arts Council England #ChangeMaker at Duckie whose other interests include filmmaking, artist/events management. Kayza is the co-founder of BlackOutLDN, whose aim is to support victims and take action against oppression suffered by People Of Colour (POC). In addition to this role Kayza is Head of Media Production at UK Black Pride. Kayza is particularly passionate about using creative outlets to give marginalised groups a voice.

PJ Samuels is a poet, educator, and LGBTI human rights activist and advocate. She is a Christian and the facilitator of 'Weather the Storm', an LGBTI refugee peer support group she started in 2015. Originally from Jamaica, she is passionately vocal about human rights, mental wellness, stigmatisation and inequalities. A rural soul, she now calls London home. 'People mystify me. Words help me frame slices of life and corral the inexplicable.'

'Nea Semba' is a non binary queer African lusophone, native to London. They have a background in creative writing and journalism, writing anonymously on slice-of-life topics as they live it, such as online activism, modernising the Black British identity through music, art and poetry, and supporting independent black artists. Nea is currently working on a podcast/blog series on 'unconventially black' creatives.

Roxanne Simone. A keen traveller and spiritual healer, Roxanne is an actor/poet who grew up in Buckinghamshire, later moved to London, and is presently globe-gliding with no fixed destination, but with heart work, poetry and creative collaboration underscoring her ongoing journey. Roxanne's poetic collaborative pieces can be found in both film and musical works, some set for release in late 2017. Roxanne's debut collection of poetry, prose, truth and beauty, *Colour Me*, is available in both paperback and e-book formats via Amazon worldwide. *Colour Me* is a journey of self-discovery and acceptance through every colour of the rainbow and beyond that heads towards the Rainbow's End. A raw, touching and truthful collection of new writing, every chapter offers shades, hues and saturations of colour that revel in and rebel against life, loss and love.

Delphine Spencer was born in Camberwell Green, South East London, to working class African Caribbean parents, and is the fourth of seven children. Her father worked for British Rail and her mother worked as an auxiliary nurse. Delphine worked as a welfare assistant and then trained as a social worker, and has worked in this field for over thirty years.

Having a love for studying Delphine has embarked on several courses, including an Advanced Diploma in Psychodynamic Counseling, a Diploma in Black Therapy, a Masters in Criminology, and a Masters in Arts Psychotherapy. She has a private practice in Brixton.

The Arts are a big part of Delphine's life and she loves going to the opera, art galleries and the theatre, she also enjoys reading and politics.

Chardine Taylor-Stone is an award-winning cultural producer and feminist activist. Her work is inspired by her experiences as a Black British working class woman having found her voice through alternative subcultures like Punk and Rockabilly. She is the founder of Black Girls Picnic, a global movement in collective self care for Black women and girls; Stop Rainbow Racism; and bangs the drums in Black feminist punk band Big Joanie.

Lightning Source UK Ltd.
Milton Keynes UK
UKHW041443090219
336905UK00001B/20/P

Also available from Team Angelica Publishing

'Reasons to Live' by Rikki Beadle-Blair
'What I Learned Today' by Rikki Beadle-Blair
'Summer in London' by Rikki Beadle-Blair

'Faggamuffin' by John R Gordon
'Colour Scheme' by John R Gordon
'Souljah' by John R Gordon

'Fairytales for Lost Children' by Diriye Osman

'Black & Gay in the UK – an anthology' edited by John R
Gordon & Rikki Beadle-Blair

'More Than – the Person Behind the Label' edited by
Gemma Van Praagh

'Tiny Pieces of Skull' by Roz Kaveney

'Slap' by Alexis Gregory

'Custody' by Tom Wainwright

'Fimí sílè Forever' by Nnanna Ikpo

'#Hashtag Lightie' by Lynette Linton

'Lives of Great Men' by Chike Frankie Edozien